MW00885411

THE ARCHEOLOGY AND HISTORY

OF

PAUL'S MISSIONARY CITIES

THE ARCHEOLOGY AND HISTORY

OF

PAUL'S MISSIONARY CITIES

by

Wilson W. Crook, III

March 2018

CreateSpace, a DBA of On-Demand Publishing, LLC
(an Amazon Company)
Charleston, South Carolina

Copyright @ 2018 by Wilson W. Crook, III.
All rights reserved.

ISBN-13: 978-1983466489

No part of this book may be reproduced or utilized in any form or by any means, electronic or mechanical, including photocopying without the permission in writing from the author. Inquiries should be addressed to Wilson W. Crook, III (dubcrook@kingwoodcable.com).

Front Cover Photo (center, top): Mosaic of the Apostle Paul, Loukas Monastery, Greece.
Front Cover Photo (center, bottom): The Temple to Apollo at Corinth.
Front Cover Photo (left, top): The Arcadian Way (Harbor Road) Leading into Ephesus.
Front Cover Photo (left, bottom): The Acrocorinth.
Front Cover Photo (right, top): The Lechaion Road (Cardo Maximus) at Corinth.
Front Cover Photo (right, bottom): Roman Forum and Shops at Thessalonica.
Back Cover Photo: The Bema (Judgment Seat) overlooking the Forum at Corinth.

INTRODUCTION

After the publication of my previous book, *The Peoples of the Bible*, a number of people have asked me, "What's next?" Coincident with these requests for more Biblical archeology

Figure 1. Mosaic of the Apostle Paul, Loukus Monastery, Greece.

writing, my wife and I made a journey with other members of our church (First Presbyterian Church of Kingwood) to Greece and Turkey following "In the Footsteps of the Apostle Paul". This trip included all of the Paul-related sites in Greece (Neopolis (Kavala), Philippi, Thessalonica, Berea, Athens and Corinth including Isthmia and Cenchreae) plus Ephesus in Turkey. We also visited Christian sites on the islands of Patmos, Rhodes (Lindos) and Crete. Previously, I have toured the island nation of Malta, which has a very strong Pauline tradition, as well as Paul's final stop in Rome. As we were visiting the above sites, it occurred to me that with just the addition of a few places in Syria and Galatia in modern day Turkey, I would have visited the sites of the entire life of the Apostle Paul and a book covering the archeology and history of his missionary cities was writing itself (Figure 1).

As with *The Peoples of the Bible*, I have utilized my notes from countless lessons given to my Present Word Adult Sunday School classes on the Book of Acts, Paul, his ministry and epistles, and the cities which he visited and worked in. In addition, over the years I have acquired a large number of books that deal with Paul's travels and, more specifically, with the archeology and history of the cities in the eastern part of Roman Empire. In preparing to write this book, I have read and re-read all of those volumes, most of which are listed in Appendix II if the reader is interested in going beyond the information presented herein.

I still receive requests from people to record my lessons dealing with Paul and other parts of the Bible, including one request that I turn them into a "Great Courses" series of videoed lectures. As I have said in the past, I have been involved in similar productions while employed by ExxonMobil, and as a consequence, I know how complex and difficult it is to effectively capture a lesson on video. Most, if not all, of my classes include visual handouts and actual archeological artifacts in addition to the spoken word. In my experience, these do not translate onto the video as well as they do as a handout in a classroom or as a printed figure in a book. Thus, again I have decided to write a book instead of making a video series.

So what is this book about? What it is NOT is a comprehensive, scientific treatise on the archeology and historicity of the cities and people that the Apostle Paul encountered through Greece and Asia Minor. I have purposefully chosen not to include specific references throughout the text in order to make the material more readable. However, I have included an Appendix at the back of this book listing a number of excellent texts covering various aspects of Paul's life and travels should the reader be moved to learn more about a particular subject. What this book IS meant to be is a relatively brief, companion reader to a Bible study class that provides some useful material about Paul, the cities, the people he ministered to and their

Figure 2. Mosaic of Paul Preaching to the Macedonians, Berea, Greece.

cultures. In this regard, I have started with Judea, specifically Jerusalem and Caesarea, where Paul both started his ministry and returned to after each of his missionary journeys. I have then proceeded more or less chronologically through the Book of Acts. Chapter 2 deals with the cities in Roman Syria and Cilicia, including Damascus, Tarsus and Antioch, the last more correctly referred to as Antioch-on-the Orontes. Chapter 3 covers Paul's First Missionary Journey to the Roman Province of Galatia and includes the cities of Antioch Pisidia, Iconium, Lystra and Derbe. Chapters 4-7 cover Paul's Second Missionary Journey through Macedonia and Greece (Neopolis and Philippi – Chapter 4; Thessalonica, Berea and Athens – Chapter 5; Corinth – Chapter 6); and then across the Aegean to Ephesus (Chapter 7) (Figure 2).

Chapter 8 covers part of Paul's final journey to Rome and includes his ministry on the islands of Rhodes (Lindos), Crete (Fair Havens) and Malta. It is surprising for as little time as Paul spent on these islands, especially compared to places like Corinth and Ephesus, how strong the Pauline tradition is in each of these islands. I conclude with a chapter on Paul's final journey to Rome (Chapter 9) and discuss the various theories of how and when Paul finally met his end. In each of these chapters, I have tried to include as many photos of the places as they are preserved today as well as photos of a few artifacts that support the Acts narrative. I have also included a table which summarizes the key dates and events for each of the discussed cities up through the end of the first century A.D.

Some may ask why are the cities of Colossae, Hierapolis and Laodicea not included in the book as Paul wrote a significant epistle to the Colossians asking that they share it with their neighboring cities (Colossians 4:16). While Paul clearly cared about the new churches in these cities, there is no evidence, either in the Book of Acts or in any of Paul's letters, that he ever visited any of them personally. He sent them letters and he sent them some of his disciples to minister to them, but he apparently did not ever personally go and evangelize in the cities. Therefore, I have made the decision to exclude these cities as they stand apart from the other ones described in this book.

In walking the Holy Land, it is often difficult to see, let alone believe, that the places you visit, now encrusted with jewels, censers, icons and the like, are the actual places walked by our Lord. With a few notable exceptions, much of what you see has to be taken on faith or you must accept that you are in the near vicinity of where an event depicted in the Bible took place. This is not the case with the cities of Paul. When you walk the streets of Philippi, Corinth or Ephesus, you stand on the stones Paul trod upon. When you stand in front of the bema (Judgment Seat) in the forum at Corinth, you are standing where the Proconsul Gallio spoke to Paul. When you sit in the giant amphitheater at Ephesus, you can almost hear the 20,000 artisans shouting down Paul with cries of "Great is Artemis of the Ephesians".

It is my sincere hope that I will be able to bring part of the story of Paul back to life in this book. If, after reading this book, the information included causes you to think differently about these ancient peoples when you read or hear the scripture, then I have accomplished my primary objective. I hope you enjoy it and to God be the Glory!

CONTENTS

FIGURES

TABLES

1 JUDEA
Jerusalem and Caesarea

Judea, specifically the cities of Jerusalem and Caesarea, is where the story of Paul in the Book of Acts both begins (Acts 7:58-60) and very nearly ends as well (Acts 23:12-15). Paul traveled to Jerusalem at least six times in his life including (1) for his advanced education under the great Jewish scholar Gamaliel, (2) after his conversion on the road to Damascus (Acts 9:26-30), (3) before his First Missionary Journey when he and Barnabas brought famine relief to the city (Acts 11:28-30; 12:25), (4) after his First Missionary Journey to attend the Council of Jerusalem (Acts 15:1-30), (5) after his Second Missionary Journey (Acts 18:21-22), and (6) after his Third and last Missionary Journey when he is arrested and tried (Acts 21:17-23:30) before appealing to Caesar for judgment and being sent to Rome. So while Paul did not spend a great deal of his ministerial life preaching in Jerusalem, the city and Judea played a pivotal role throughout the Apostle's life.

JERUSALEM

Paul was born to a reasonably well-to-do Jewish family in Tarsus, a city to the north of Judea in the Roman Province of Cilicia. We do not know the precise date of his birth, but many scholars place it around 5 A.D. based on the fact that church tradition places Paul near the age of 60 at the time of his death. We know something of his family lineage and early life based on the comments he makes later in his letters to the Philippians and to the Galatians:

"If someone else thinks they have reasons to put confidence in the flesh, I have more: circumcised on the eighth day, of the people of Israel, of the tribe of Benjamin, a Hebrew of Hebrews; in regard to the law, a Pharisee; as for zeal, persecuting the church; as for righteousness based on the law, faultless" (Philippians 3:4-6)

"I advanced in Judaism beyond many among my people of the same age, for I was more zealous for the traditions of my ancestors" (Galatians 1:14)

In these few sentences, Paul tells us that he was born to a Jewish family that kept strict adherence to the law. He was circumcised on the eighth day after birth as was prescribed by the law. He knew he was of the tribe of Benjamin - an unusual fact. Many Jews by the first century A.D. did not know their original tribal affiliation as during and after the Babylonian captivity (586-539 B.C.), family identity began to supersede that of tribal (see Ezra 2). Not only was Paul from the tribe of Benjamin, but his Jewish birth name was Saul, named for Israel's first king, who was also from the tribe of Benjamin. Paul further states that he was "a Hebrew of Hebrews". This is probably not a reference to his family's strict adherence to the law as much as it likely means that his family spoke and wrote the Hebrew language, again something that not everyone who was a Jew could do in the first century A.D.

Paul further identifies himself as a Pharisee, with great zeal in persecuting the (Christian) church. The Pharisees (meaning the "separated ones") as a group stem from the second century B.C., during the Jewish (Hasmonean) rule of Palestine. Unlike the ruling class and priests that made up the Sadducees, the Pharisees refused to compromise and accept any form of Hellenization that had been imposed on the region after the death of Alexander the Great. The Pharisees were from more common stock than the Sadducees, but were highly educated, ultra-religious and legalistically focused. Rather than exclusively worship in the Temple, the Pharisees focused their attention on knowledge of the scriptures and worship in the local synagogues. They believed in both the written law as well as the oral law tradition. They believed in both angels and demons and in an afterlife in which God would punish the wicked and reward the righteous, of which the most righteous of all, of course, were the Pharisees. Not all the Pharisees were unaccepting, but in the end, they could not reconcile Jesus' actions and claims with their own understanding of piety and godliness which led to the many encounters between Jesus and the Pharisees as recorded throughout the gospels. These confrontations, often very violent, continued after Jesus' death and resurrection between the Pharisees and the early apostles trying to spread the word of the Gospel. Paul's early description of himself and the role he played in persecuting the early Christian church fits perfectly with the doctrine of a highly educated Pharisee of the first century A.D.

While Tarsus was known as a city that had a substantial Jewish population and a high regard for education, anyone who wanted to become a Pharisee of high esteem would have continued his education in Jerusalem under one of the great teachers that taught in and around the Temple. In the first century A.D., Jewish education somewhat mirrored that of Roman schools, with the exception that classes were taught by a local Pharisee or Rabbi in the synagogue. A basic education consisting of what we would call primary or elementary school subjects was taught mostly to male children starting near the age of seven through about age 12-13. This would be the equivalent to what we would associate as a sixth grade education and would consist of basic reading, writing and elementary mathematics. Both the reading and writing would have been from the scriptures and probably would have been taught in both Aramaic and Greek, the two *lingua francas* of the day for most of the Ancient Middle East. Paul may have had some schooling in Hebrew, although it is more likely that he learned the language from it being spoken in his household.

Formal schooling ended for most children at age 12-13, primarily because this was the age that young boys formally entered the community as men (*bar mitzvah*) and as such, were expected to assist the family in making a living. By this age, most children had been given the basic fundamentals of education that they needed to function in the Roman business world. Only children from very well-to-do families, who did not need the immediate income from their work, were sent on to Secondary School. In the Roman world of the first century A.D., Secondary (and later Oratory) school consisted of advanced reading and writing as well as some history and science, but was primarily focused on logic, rhetoric and public speaking. These were the key skill sets needed for a life either in politics or administration / public service. Advanced Jewish schools had a similar philosophy but the subjects were restricted to the scriptures and the oral and written law of the *Talmud*. Jewish educators (Rabbis) taught by posing a series of philosophical questions about how the law should be applied to daily life, thereby requiring the students to think and compose their responses in an orderly, logical manner.

The most respected of all Jewish educators in the first century A.D. was Gamaliel the Elder. Gamaliel held the titles of *Nasi* (Prince of the Sanhedrin) and *Rabban* (Our Master). In the Jewish *Mishnah*, the oral tradition that was later transcribed, it is written that he was the greatest teacher in all the history of Judaism:

> *"Since Rabban Gamaliel the Elder has died, there has been no more reverence for the law, and purity and piety died out at the same time."*

Gamaliel's unquestioned authority on religious law is supported by two anecdotes in the *Mishnah* which state that he was consulted by "the King and the Queen" on matters of rituals. We do not know which king and queen this refers to but is likely to either be Herod Agrippa I and his wife Cypros, or Herod Agrippa II and his sister/consort Bernice. Gamaliel was also of the tribe of Benjamin, so it was only natural that a bright young student like Paul should journey to Jerusalem to study under the greatest of teachers in the Jewish world.

Assuming Paul was about 13 years old when he moved from Tarsus to Jerusalem to continue his education, that would place him in the city around 18 A.D. during the reign of the Emperor Tiberius. We do not know how long Paul stayed and studied under Gamaliel, but from all accounts Paul was one of his brightest, most able students who received what we would term as his High School, University and Post-Graduate degrees from the master educator. Paul himself states that, although born in Tarsus, he was brought up in Jerusalem "at the feet of Gamaliel, and taught according to the perfect manner of the law of the fathers" (Acts 22:3). Gamaliel reportedly classified his students into four groups using a metaphor of a fish:

1. A ritually impure fish: one who has memorized everything, but has no understanding and is the son of poor parents.

2. A ritually pure fish: one who has learned and understood everything, and is from rich parents.

3. A fish from the Jordan River: one who has learned everything but does not know how to apply it.

4. A fish from the Mediterranean: one who has learned everything and knows how to respond.

We can only assume that Paul fit either into category two or four, although there is some scholarly debate on the nature of his relationship with his master teacher. In Acts 5:38-39, Gamaliel counsels the Sanhedrin to leave the apostles alone rather than punishing them, stating that if their message (the Gospel) is not from God, it will soon disappear; however, if the message of the apostles was from God, then it would be wise to refrain from punishment and be on God's side. This message of religious patience and tolerance contrasts greatly with Paul's zeal at pursuing and punishing the apostles and the early followers of the church.

The first mention of Paul in the Bible comes at the end of the story of the Apostle Stephen, when he is martyred by stoning (Acts 7:58-60). Paul is depicted as a Pharisee on the side of Caiaphas the High Priest and the rest of the Sanhedrin who are trying to suppress the teaching of Jesus' Gospel. Paul is portrayed as a young but influential Pharisee who is not only knowledgeable, but a recognized expert in Jewish law. Assuming Jesus was crucified around 30 A.D., scholars place the stoning of Stephen sometime shortly thereafter in 31-32 A.D. If so, then Paul would have been living, studying and working in Jerusalem for almost half of his life at the time. As such, he would have had an intimate knowledge of the city and its environs, and especially of the Temple.

The Roman Empire was based on order: territorial order achieved and maintained through the strength of its Legions; civil order administered and enforced through a codex of laws; and architectural order created by the systematic use of urban planning which was copied all across the Empire – from Britain, Gaul and Germany in the north to Asia Minor and Palestine in the east. Wherever possible, Roman cities were laid out into a uniform north-south, east-west Cartesian coordinate system. However, some ancient and already developed cities that later became Roman possessions were allowed to continue as they were until a natural or man-made disaster allowed the city to be rebuilt along the Roman urban model. In this regard, Jerusalem, with its hundreds of narrow, winding streets, must have been a night-mare for the Roman authorities.

The Romans were great admirers of Greek education and culture. Nowhere was this more evident than in the respect held for Hippodamus of Miletus, the father of modern urban planning. Hippodamus was the inventor of the "Hippodamian Plan", or the grid plan for the layout of cities. Hippodamus lived in the fifth century B.C. during the apex of Classical Greece. His plans for Greek cities were characterized by order and regularity in contrast to the chaos and warrens of narrow streets common to many cities of the period. He is seen as the originator of the idea that urban city planning could embody a rational sense of order and not be subject to the whims of random street and building construction.

Hippodamus' plan envisioned that a perfect city would be inhabited by no more than 10,000 men (free male citizens), with a corresponding overall population including women, children and slaves of about 50,000 people. He divided his city's population into three classes: soldiers, artisans and husbandmen (farmers) with the land also divided into three main purposes: sacred, public and private. Hippodamus' urban plan consisted of two wide main streets that intersected at right angles near the center of the city. At this intersection would be the main market or *agora*. Shops and other public facilities would line these main thoroughfares while private residences were placed in the suburban areas away from the city center. Sacred buildings would either be located near the main public areas or on top of prominent geographic features that were not strictly reserved for the city's defense. This basic design for a city is still in use today and can be seen in virtually every country worldwide.

The order and basic simplicity of Hippodamus' design strongly appealed to the Romans, especially to the military with regard to their camps and fortifications. Accordingly, Roman military camps or *Castra* (singular *Castrum*) were built all across the Empire to the basic design of the Hippodamian Plan. A major north-south street (Main Street or the *Via Principalis*) was constructed with side streets at right angles. The primary side street was called the *Via Praetoria* because it was interrupted at the intersection with the Via Principalis by the *Praetorium* or central headquarters. This building was called the Praetorium because it housed the *Praetor* (First Officer) or Commander of the camp. The parade / drill ground was also located near the camp center. Workshops, bakeries, baths, commissaries, etc. lined the main street with the soldiers housed in billets that filled the remaining quadrants of the rectangular pattern. Earthen or stone walls (depending on the length of time the unit was billeted at a given camp) were constructed around the edges of the rectangle and guard towers would also be placed periodically around the perimeter. Typically, four gates were constructed. The main gate or *Porta Praetoria*, would usually be either to the left or right of the camp center as traveling through this gate would bring one to the Praetorium. The back gate was known as the *Porta Decumana* while the other two gates were known as the *Porta Principalis Dextra* and the *Porta Principalis Sinistra*.

While designed to be a temporary "city", many of these military camps later developed into more permanent towns, such as Eboracum (modern York, U.K.), Colonia Agrippina (Cologne, Germany), and Augusta Praetoria (Aosta, Italy).

The Romans applied the Castrum model to their cities across the Empire. Where possible, they built a major north-south road as the entrance way into the city. This road was known as the *Cardo Maximus*, or main road. The Cardo Maximus served as the hinge axis for the city and was frequently lined with shops. As such, the Cardo Maximus was frequently colonnaded with awnings suspended to provide travelers and shoppers with protection from both the sun and rain. At the entrance way to the city on the Cardo Maximus would be a gate structure. Sometimes the gate was relatively modest; in other cities, especially those that enjoyed Imperial favor, the city entrance could be monumentally impressive.

At a right angle to the Cardo Maximus, and usually near its mid-point in length, would be a major east-west street known as the *Decamus Maximus*. The Decamus Maximus served as a secondary main street and was also typically lined with shops. Depending on the size of the city, other east-west side streets could be built but they were usually narrower than either the Decamus Maximus or the Cardo Maximus. While the Cardo Maximus was the preferred main street for a city, sometimes due to variances in geography the Decamus Maximus served as the major thoroughfare. For example, at Philippi in Macedonia, the city was built along the *Via Egnatia*, which served as the major road connecting Italy in the west to Constantinople in the east. As such, this east-west road (technically a Decamus Maximus) served as the Cardo Maximus for the city.

At or near the intersection of the two main streets would be the central market place, or *forum* (a*gora* in Greek; literally "assembly" or "meeting place"). This area was often lined with shops on all sides, with the entrance way often sheltered by a colonnaded breeze way, forming a *stoa*. Shops were often multi-storied structures, with the main or forum-level room being the principal store. A smaller upper story was used as living quarters for the shop owners or for their slaves whose job was to protect the shop after closing. If the shop sold easily perishable food (meat, fish) or wine, the shop keepers would often construct a lower floor down into the bedrock which would keep the products cool until moved to the main shop upstairs for sale.

During his travels later in his life, Paul would become intimately familiar with this uniform city design as it was repeated in Syria, Galatia, Ephesus, Philippi, Thessalonica, Berea, Athens and Corinth. However, Jerusalem was already a major city by the time the Romans absorbed it in 63 B.C. Almost all of the buildings in the city were constructed from blocks of local Jerusalem limestone (as is modern Jerusalem today) as opposed to mud brick or wood which could be easily torn down and removed. Therefore, there was little the Romans could do to change the city into the uniform model design described above.

Table 1. Key Dates and Events for Jerusalem through the First Century A.D.

Date	Event
ca. 1000 B.C.	David captures the Jebusite city of Jerusalem and makes it his new capital
ca. 966 B.C.	Solomon starts construction on the Temple
ca. 701 B.C.	Jerusalem survives a siege by the Assyrian King Sennacherib
ca. 587-586 B.C.	Babylonian King Nebuchadnezzar lays siege to Jerusalem; destroys the city and Solomon's Temple
539-331B.C.	Jerusalem under Persian Empire control
ca. 520-515 B.C.	Temple rebuilt on a smaller scale by the Jews returning from Babylonian exile
331-160 B.C.	Jerusalem under Greek (Macedonian and Seleucid) control
167-160 B.C.	Maccabean revolt against Greek (Seleucid) rule
160-63 B.C.	Hasmonean (Jewish) rule in Jerusalem
63 B.C.	Jerusalem brought into the Roman Empire
ca. 19-10 B.C.	Herod rebuilds the Temple; dedicated in ca. 10 B.C. but work continued until 66 A.D.
ca. 30 A.D.	Approximate date of Jesus' crucifixion; first preaching of the Christian Gospel by the Apostles in the Temple and its courts (Acts 3-4)
ca. 31 A.D.	Stoning of Stephen; witnessed by Paul (Acts 9)
ca. 34-35 A.D.	Paul returns to Jerusalem after his conversion and spends a fortnight with Peter and James
ca. 41-44 A.D.	Under Herod Agrippa I, Jerusalem expands northward to encompass the site of Jesus' crucifixion and burial
ca. 45-46 A.D.	Paul and Barnabas visit Jerusalem to offer famine relief; Paul meets with Peter, John and James (Acts 11)
ca. 49 A.D.	Paul returns to Jerusalem after his First Missionary Journey; Council of Jerusalem (Acts 15)
ca. 52-53 A.D.	Paul returns to Jerusalem after his Second Missionary Journey (Acts 18)
ca. 57 A.D.	Paul, Luke and companions return to Jerusalem after his Third Missionary Journey; Paul is arrested and then removed to Caesarea for trial (Acts 21:17-23:30)
ca. 62 A.D.	James (brother of Jesus) is martyred
ca. 66-70 A.D.	Jewish revolt against Rome; Jerusalem is besieged and captured by Titus; Herod's Temple is destroyed

Jerusalem was founded during the Bronze Age by the Jebusites, one of seven Canaanite tribes that originally inhabited Palestine. David captured the city around 1000 B.C. and made it the capital for the new state of Israel (Table 1). The city changed hands several times having been conquered by the Babylonians in 586 B.C., then controlled by the Persians after the fall of Babylon in 539 B.C., and finally by the Macedonians and the Seleucid Greeks until 167 B.C. After a brief period of Jewish (Hasmonean) rule, Jerusalem was incorporated into the Roman Empire in 63 B.C..

By the first century A.D., Jerusalem was a complex warren of winding narrow streets. Nowhere was this more evident than in the Old City, the so-called City of David, that lay immediately south of the Temple Mount (Figure 3). Moreover, the city was honeycombed with tunnels and caverns which provided shelter for those who wished to hide from the authorities. The people of the first century A.D. lived with a lot of filth in their lives as sanitation was relatively poor. In large cities like Jerusalem, daily waste would have been dumped in the spaces between houses. It was then collected and taken out through the Dung Gate to an area outside of the city where it was dumped and burned in a

Figure 3. Model of First Century A.D. Jerusalem, Israel Museum, Jerusalem.

continual fire. The locals referred to this area of Jerusalem as *Gehenna* or hell because of the perpetual stench. As a result, home owners always placed their windows on the second floor of the buildings – above the smell of the waste. Spices were used to perfume houses, although the smell of olive oil would have been pervasive. Perfumes were popular to cover up body odor; there is little hard evidence the people of Palestine either made or used much soap. Hair styles were typically short and beards were well trimmed. Judging from burial inscriptions found outside the city (cemeteries were always placed "in the wilderness" beyond city walls because of disease and the law that stated that corpses were ritually unclean), the typical life expectancy of a male in first century A.D. Palestine was only about 29 years of age.

Framing the skyline of the city was the Temple Mount which was crowned with the Second, or Herod's, Temple, the holiest site in all of Judaism. The Temple had originally been planned by King David but was built by his son Solomon sometime between 966-959 B.C. The First, or Solomon's, Temple, stood until it was destroyed by King Nebuchadnezzar and the Babylonian army in 586 B.C. After their return from exile sometime after 539 B.C., the surviving Jews rebuilt the Temple, completing the project around 516 B.C. Unlike Solomon's Temple, specific dimensions of the rebuilt Second Temple are not given in the Bible but many of the older people who had seen and remembered Solomon's Temple cried at the Second Temple's dedication as apparently it was only a shadow of the original structure (Ezra 3:12-13).

Figure 4. Model of Herod's Temple, Israel Museum, Jerusalem.

This temple stood for the next five centuries until it was greatly expanded and rebuilt by Herod the Great (Figure 4).

Initially Rome allowed limited Jewish rule over the area of Palestine but the persistence of revolts against the Empire led to Rome placing its own king on the throne of Judea. This action began the succession of the family of Herod the Great, who, along with a series of Roman procurators, controlled Palestine for the next century.

Herod the Great was born around 71-74 B.C., the second son of Antipater the Idumean, a high-ranking official under the Jewish King Hyrcanus II. Herod's mother was Cypros, a Nabatean Princess from Petra. At age 25, he was appointed the local Governor for Galilee by the Roman Governor of the region. The brutality of Herod's rule was condemned by the Sanhedrin (the governing body of the Jewish people) and he was generally despised for being an Idumean (a descendant of the Edomite people) and not an ethnic Jew. In the aftermath of the assassination of Julius Caesar, the young Herod was forced to choose to which side in the Roman civil war he would pledge his allegiance. Initially siding with the conspirators Cassius and Brutus, he quickly changed sides as the war began to favor the side of Marc Anthony and Octavian (later Augustus Caesar). Octavian appointed Herod to be Tetrarch of Galilee but the Jewish people forced Herod to flee to Rome in exile. There, Octavian and the Roman Senate proclaimed Herod "King of the Jews" in 37 B.C.

Herod returned to Palestine with his Roman allies, routed the opposing forces and reclaimed his throne. He became close friends with both Marc Anthony and Cleopatra. However, when Augustus defeated the forces of Anthony and Cleopatra at the Battle of Actium in 31 B.C. and became the first Roman Emperor, Herod quickly switched sides again and pledged loyalty to the new Caesar. He was rewarded by Augustus by being re-confirmed King of Judea in 30 B.C. While Herod adopted all of the worship practices of his Jewish subjects, he continued to suffer from the fact that most of the Jews did not consider him to be one of them. To help remedy this, Herod married Mariamne, the granddaughter of the last Jewish King, Hyrcanus II. Herod already had one wife, Doris, at the time and he would marry another seven women in his lifetime, and at least seven of his wives would bear him children. Herod was paranoid about losing his throne and he constantly perceived plots against him from his wives, and, more especially, from his sons. As a result, he had three of his sons killed between 7 B.C. and 4 B.C. So ruthless was Herod towards his family that the Emperor Augustus once remarked, "It is better to be Herod's pig than his son."

Aside from his brutality and paranoia, Herod the Great was known as a great architect and builder, having built the fortress on the mountain top at Masada, the fortress at Herodium, a palace around the springs at Jericho, and the port of Caesarea Maritima with its artificial harbor (the construction completed with revolutionary quick-drying cement under the sea). But his greatest building achievement was the complete rebuilding of the Second Temple in

Jerusalem (Figures 5-8). To enlarge the Temple grounds, Herod's builders constructed a new platform that completely spanned Mount Moriah. The Second Temple itself was covered in gold, ivory and cedar, with a series of outer courts built on top of the new platform. The initial work on expanding the Temple Mount was completed between 20 B.C. and 10 B.C., but the final completion of all the rebuilding was not completed until ca. 60 A.D. Some of the stones used in building the platform's foundation weighed over 500 tons – the heaviest known building stones ever used. The great Western Stone is 48.6 feet in length by 9.8 feet height with

Figure 5. The Temple Mount Today, Jerusalem.

Figure 6. Western or Wailing Wall, Jerusalem.

Figure 7. Detail of the Western Wall.

Figure 8. The Great Western Stone in the Western Wall of the Temple Mount, Jerusalem.

an estimated width of 10.8 feet and weighs an estimated 570 tons (Figure 8). So impressive was the new structure that it was widely considered to be the single most impressive building in the entire Roman world until the construction of the Colosseum. Today, all that remain of Herod's

Temple are the stones making up part of the western side of the Temple Mount, known as the Western or "Wailing" Wall (see Figures 6-7).

Herod's Temple, which would have been the Temple of both Jesus and Paul, was so ornate and elaborate that when the Romans sacked Jerusalem at the end of the Jewish War (66-70 A.D.), the gold and ivory stripped from the structure completely financed the construction of the world famous Colosseum in Rome.

It is unknown if Paul on any of his trips to Jerusalem after his conversion on the road to Damascus, visited some of the sites associated with Jesus' life, such as the Mount of Olives (Jesus' ascension to heaven) or Golgotha (the site of Jesus' crucifixion and burial). It is very likely that he did but we have no record of such visits either in the Book of Acts or in any of Paul's letters.

CAESAREA

The other major Judean city which Paul frequently visited was Caesarea Maritima, located on the Mediterranean coast about halfway between the modern cities of Tel Aviv and Haifa. While Israel has an extensive Mediterranean coastline, heavy siltation from both wind-blown African sands and from discharge from the Nile Delta has resulted in few natural harbors. As a consequence, in 22 B.C. Herod the Great decided to create a new harbor to provide his kingdom with an entrance way for imported goods as well as a fast communication link to the rest of the Roman Mediterranean (Table 2).

Herod chose the location for his new seaport at the site of an old Phoenician port known as Strabo's (or Strato's) Tower. Construction on the port and an adjacent city began in 22 B.C. and was completed in 10 B.C. The city was named "Caesarea" in honor of Caesar Augustus (Herod was never shy about currying favor with the Roman powers of the day) and it became not only the major port for Judea but also the Roman political and administrative capital for the province (Table 2).

Caesarea was everything that Jerusalem was not. Jerusalem was an old city by the first century A.D.; Caesarea was brand new. Jerusalem was in a remote place in the Judean Highlands; Caesarea was along the coast with links to rest of the Roman Empire. Jerusalem was the center of Judaism and Jewish worship in the Temple; Caesarea was the commercial and

Table 2. Key Dates and Events for Caesarea through the First Century A.D.

Date	Event
22 B.C.	Herod the Great founds Caesarea (naming it in honor of Caesar Augustus) on the site of Strabo's Tower; purpose of the city is to provide Judea with a major port and a communication link to Roman Empire
10 B.C.	Construction is completed; city dedicated to Augustus
6 A.D.	Caesarea named as capital of Roman province of Palestine
26-36 A.D.	Pontius Pilate serves as Procurator of Palestine
ca. 38 A.D.	Peter visits Caesarea and converts the Roman Centurion Cornelius and his family (Acts 10)
44 A.D.	Death of Herod Agrippa I (Acts 12)
52-59 A.D.	Marcus Antonius Felix serves as Procurator of Palestine
57-59 A.D.	Paul removed from Jerusalem to Caesarea where he remains in prison for two years (Acts 23-25)
59-62 A.D.	Porcius Festus serves as Procurator of Palestine
66 A.D.	Jewish revolt begins in Caesarea; spreads throughout Palestine
66-70 A.D.	Jewish War in Palestine; ends with the capture of Jerusalem and the destruction of the Temple

administrative center of Roman Palestine with temples to pagan gods, amphitheaters and a hippodrome. The two cities could not have been more of a contrast to one another. Luke portrays this extreme difference in his account of Peter's travel to Caesarea to visit the Roman Centurion Cornelius and his family (Acts 10-11:18).

Caesarea was also a major engineering marvel. To construct the artificial harbor, Herod's engineers built two massive, curved harbor walls reaching out into the sea (Figure 9). These were constructed using massive limestone blocks joined together by a relatively new invention, concrete. The Romans did not have a quick-setting concrete as is used in industry today; rather they used hydrated lime – created by heating limestone ($CaCO_3$) and driving off CO_2 to form lime (CaO). Lime does not act like concrete on its own and will only form cement when mixed with water and the volcanic rock, pumice (also known as "pozzolan"). When lime and water are mixed with pumice, which is largely amorphous silica, nearly all of the lime is converted to Calcium Silicate Hydrate or "C-S-H". In modern Portland Cement, the hydraulic reaction that produces the C-S-H binder happens very quickly without the need of pumice but at a cost. A deleterious by-product, calcium hydroxide $(Ca(OH_2)$ is created which contributes nothing to the strength and durability of the concrete. Over time, calcium hydroxide migrates out of the cement via a fine-grain pore system leaving behind an interlaced network of holes that compromises the density and allows for the ingress of water containing sulfates, chlorides and other chemicals which over time attack the concrete. This means that modern concrete, while easy to produce and quick-setting, has a finite lifetime.

Figure 9. Remains of Herod's Harbor at Caesarea, Israel.

Roman concrete, on the other hand, has been shown to last not just for centuries but for millennia. The addition of pumice (pozzolan) ignites a secondary reaction that changes almost all of the deleterious calcium hydroxide into additional C-S-H. This secondary C-S-H densifies and further strengthens the concrete, welding it into an almost impermeable matrix. At Caesarea, large wooden frames were built around the sunken limestone blocks which were then filled with pozzolanic concrete. Most of the original harbor walls lie offshore today, submerged just below sea level but still easily visible. The southern harbor breakwater measured 200 feet wide by 2,000 feet

Figure 10. Remains of the Major Aqueduct System at Caesarea, Israel. (Photo Courtesy of Denis P. Wolf)

long and at its end was a large tower which probably served as a lighthouse.

In addition to forming a breakwater and harbor wall, Herod's engineers designed a special sluice gate at the harbor entrance which prevented the harbor from becoming silted up and unusable, something that would plague other first century A.D. cities such as Ephesus. They further devised a sewage system which took advantage of the tides and flushed away the city's waste materials twice a day. To ensure an abundant supply of fresh water to the city, a tunnel and a major aqueduct system were built to bring water from permanent springs six miles away at the base of Mount Carmel (Figure 10). A second aqueduct running side-by-side with the Herodian structure was built by the Emperor Hadrian ca. 130 A.D.

Figure 11. Roman Theater at Caesarea, Israel. (Photo Courtesy of Denis P. Wolf)

Figure 12. Roman Hippodrome at Caesarea, Israel.

The city of Caesarea was built inland from the harbor and laid out on a standard Roman Cartesian system with a north-south Cardo Maximus and a number of intersecting east-west streets (*Decamani*). Shops bringing items from Egypt, Asia Minor, Greece and Rome lined the major streets. Herod built a major defensive wall encircling the city which encompassed about 8,000 acres and included a theater (*odeon*), a *hippodrome*, and a major temple to Augustus (*Augusteum*) (Figures 11-12). The latter is obscured today

Figure 13. Remains of Herod's Promontory Palace at Caesarea, Israel. (Photo Courtesy of Denis P. Wolf)

by the remains of a Crusader church to St. Peter but is believed to have originally been about 100 x 165 feet in size. The theater had a seating capacity of about 4,000 and is still used for performances today. The hippodrome is believed to have had a seating capacity for about 15,000 patrons. At its peak in the first century A.D., Caesarea was believed to have had as many as 30,000 inhabitants.

Jutting out into the sea south of the harbor is the Promontory Palace, which may well have been the location of King Herod's palace. This palace was renowned for its beautiful bathing pool located near its center (Figure 13). After his death in approximately 4 B.C., the palace became the functional residence and seat of governance for the Roman Procurators of Judea including the Biblical figures of Pontius Pilate, Marcus Antonius Felix, and Porcius Festus.

In 1961, near the theater, Italian archeologists found a 32 x 25 inch block of limestone which contained a significant partial inscription. The inscription reads:

[DIS AUGUSTI]S TIBERIE-
UM
[PON]TIUS PILATATUS
[PRAEF]ECTUS
IUDA[EA]E
[FECIT D]E [DICAVIT]
To the Divine Tiberieum
Pontius Pilate
Prefect of Judea
Has Dedicated This

Figure 14. Pontius Pilate Inscription Found at Caesarea in 1961.

The inscription was probably part of a temple dedicated to the Emperor Tiberius and dates to the time Pilate was Procurator (Prefect) of Judea (26-36 A.D.) (Figure 14).

The Apostle Paul visited Caesarea on several occasions including after his conversion on the road to Damascus and return visit to the apostles in Jerusalem, after the Council of Jerusalem, and after his Second and Third Missionary Journeys. Each time, Paul's visit was short, primarily using Caesarea as a port to enter Judea and travel to Jerusalem or to catch a ship to return to Asia and his ministry. However, at the end of his Third Missionary Journey, Paul traveled to Jerusalem where he was accused of blasphemy and put on trial by the Sanhedrin. Realizing that he was not going to receive a fair hearing with the Jews, Paul appealed to the Roman Procurator at the time, Marcus Antonius Felix, to be judged under Roman law. As a Roman citizen, Paul had the legal right to appeal his case through the Roman legal system up to a hearing before Caesar. Felix had a detachment of 200 soldiers, 70 cavalrymen and 200 spearmen escort Paul under guard from Jerusalem to Caesarea (Acts 23:23).

For the next two years (ca. 57-59 A.D.), Paul was held at Herod's old palace in Caesarea, by this time being used by the Roman procurators. Paul was kept nominally under guard but was allowed visitation rights so his friends could see to his needs (Acts 22:23). During this time, Felix visited Paul on a number of occasions (Acts 24:22-26). At the end of two years, Felix was called back to Rome and was replaced by a new Procurator, Porcius Festus. Unlike Felix who had a Jewish wife, Festus had neither ties to Judea nor any experience in dealing with Jewish legal matters. Faced with the prospect of being returned to Jerusalem to stand judgment before the Sanhedrin, Paul cited his right as a Roman citizen to appeal his case before the Emperor in Rome. To this request, Festus replied, "You have appealed to Caesar. To Caesar you will go!" (Acts 25:12). This begins the final part of Paul's life and his journey to Rome.

Interestingly, after making his appeal to Caesar, Festus discussed Paul's case with King Herod Agrippa II and his wife/consort, Bernice. After hearing Paul speak, Agrippa commented to Festus, "This man is not doing anything that deserves death or imprisonment . . . This man could have been set free if he had not appealed to Caesar" (Acts 26:31-32).

2 SYRIA AND CILICIA
Damascus, Tarsus and Antioch-On-The-Orontes

After the execution of Stephen, Paul (then known by his Jewish name, Saul), approached the High Priest Caiaphas in order to obtain warrants for the arrests of other followers of Jesus. Paul had heard that there was a growing church of Christians in Damascus and he wished to go find and arrest those blasphemers and bring them back to Jerusalem for judgment:

"Meanwhile Saul, still breathing out threats to murder the Lord's disciples, went to the high priest and requested letters from him to the synagogues in Damascus, so that if he found anyone belonging to the Way, either men or women, he could bring them as prisoners to Jerusalem." (Acts 9:1-2)

Paul would have traveled to Damascus along the Via Maris (Way of the Sea), the ancient overland trade route that connected Egypt to Mesopotamia. Paul would have gone down from Jerusalem to the coast to Joppa, where the road traveled north from Joppa to Dor, then turned northeast through the Jezreel Valley to the Sea of Galilee. At the north end of the Sea of Galilee, Paul would have passed through the small fishing village of Capernaum, which had been the home to Jesus and His apostles throughout His ministry. East of Capernaum, the Via Maris wound its way up through the region now known as the Golan Heights, and finally onto a downhill plain that led to Damascus. The total trip from Jerusalem to Damascus was about 150 miles and would have taken Paul and his guards about a week to make.

About 10 miles west of Damascus, near a small rise known as Kaukab Hill, an event occurred that would forever change the young man's life:

"As he was going along, approaching Damascus, suddenly a light from heaven flashed around them. He fell to the ground and heard a voice saying to him, 'Saul, Saul, why are you persecuting me?' So he replied, 'Who are you, Lord?' He replied, 'I am Jesus whom you are persecuting! But stand up and enter the city and you will be told what you must do'. Now the men who were traveling with him stood there speechless, because they heard the voice but saw no one.

So Saul got up from the ground, but although his eyes were open, he could see nothing. Leading him by the hand, his companions brought him into Damascus. For three days he could not see, and he neither ate nor drank anything." (Acts 9:3-9)

Table 3. Key Dates and Events for Damascus Through the First Century A.D.

Date	Event
ca. 2400-2250 B.C.	Clay tablets found in Ebla refer to the city of "Dimashqi", believed to be Damascus
ca. 1400 B.C.	Egyptian inscription refers to "Timasqu" (Damascus) to be under Egyptian control
ca. 1300 B.C.	The Amarna letters from Egypt refer to "Timaasghi" (Damascus) as periodically being under Hittite control
ca. 1250-1000 B.C.	Damascus is a major City-State in the Aramean Kingdom of Syria
ca. 1000-960 B.C.	Damascus under the control of David and Solomon
ca. 850-750 B.C.	Damascus and Syria in constant conflict with Northern Kingdom of Israel
ca. 732 B.C.	Damascus destroyed by Assyrian King Tiglath-Pileser
612-539 B.C.	Damascus controlled by the Neo-Babylonian Empire
539-333 B.C.	Damascus controlled by the Persian Empire
333-85 B.C.	Damascus controlled by Greeks (Macedonians) and Seleucid Greeks
85-64 B.C.	Damascus controlled by Nabatean King Aretas III
64 B.C.	Damascus captured by Romans (Pompey) and incorporated into Roman Empire
ca. 31-35 A.D.	Paul's conversion on the road outside Damascus; after preaching the Gospel, he escapes in a basket through the city wall (Acts 9); after spending time in the Arabian desert, Paul briefly returns to Damascus and then departs for Jerusalem (Galatians 1)
67 A.D.	18,000 Jews massacred in Damascus during First Jewish War with Rome

DAMASCUS

Paul was taken by his men into Damascus to the house of a Jew named Judas who lived on "Straight Street" (Acts 9:11). Damascus lays claim to be the oldest continuously inhabited city in the world (Table 3). Written records dating from as early as 2400 B.C. from the Canaanite archive at Ebla refer to the city as "Dimashqi", believed to be Damascus. Scholars believe the city is much older than that with its founding being possibly as early as the Copper Age (ca. 3400-4600 B.C.) or even the Neolithic Age (ca. 4600+ B.C.). Damascus is located at the confluence of two rivers, the Amana and the Pharpar. It sits on a high plateau and is sheltered by the Anti Lebanon Mountains, which provide it with rain and block the hot desert winds. As such, Damascus has always been an oasis on the edge of the desert and a favorable place to live.

Damascus was the main city of the Syrian league of city-states that formed the Aramean Kingdom. It has had a long relationship with Israel, often adversarial, with each nation periodically having superiority over the other. Damascus was completely destroyed and rebuilt several times, first by the Neo-Assyrians under Tiglath-Pileser III in 732 B.C. and later by the Neo-Babylonian Empire under Nebuchadnezzar. The Roman General Pompey the Great captured the city in 64 B.C. and it remained under Roman control for the next 6 centuries. Under Roman rule, Damascus was incorporated into a collective of relatively independent city-states known as the Decapolis and placed within the Province of Syria.

Figure 15. The Straight Street, Now Covered, in Damascus, Syria. (Photo Courtesy of VV Travel, Russia)

The Romans completely redesigned Damascus and created the established north-south (Cardo Maximus), east-west (Cardo Decamus) grid layout, with the main east-west road being about twice as long as the Cardo Maximus. This east-west road was part of the pre-existing Via Maris and because it was unbending for nearly a mile in length, it became known as Straight Street (or the Via Recta).

As was typical of most Roman cities, Straight Street was colonnaded and lined with shops. Recently, the Syrian Government has re-created an ancient look by building a spectacular wide colonnaded thoroughfare which stands in stark contrast to the narrow winding streets in the rest of the city (Figure 15).

In the first century A.D., Damascus was populated by a mixture of Syrians, Greeks and Jews. The Jewish population was substantial and boasted a number of synagogues. The fact that Paul's local contact, Judas, had a house on Straight Street shows that he was a man of significant means and importance. Paul remained in Judas' house for three days, stunned and probably not knowing if he was going to live or die. His strong personal belief that the Gospel story told by the apostles of Jesus was a complete myth and must be violently eradicated had suddenly been shattered by the visitation of this same Jesus on the road outside Damascus. Paul's life was about to receive another shock:

"Now there was a disciple in Damascus named Ananias. The Lord said to him in a vision, 'Ananias' and he replied, 'Here I am Lord'. Then the Lord told him, 'Get up and go to the street called Straight, and at Judas' house look for a man from Tarsus named Saul. For he is praying, and he has seen in a vision a man named Ananias come in and place his hands on him so that he may see again'. But Ananias replied, 'Lord, I have heard from many people about this man, how much harm he has done to your saints in Jerusalem, and he has authority from the chief priests to imprison all who call on your name.' But the Lord said to him, 'Go because this man is my chosen instrument to carry my name before Gentiles and kings and the people of Israel. For I will show him how much he must suffer for the sake of my name'. So Ananias departed and entered the house, placed his hands on Saul and said, 'Brother Saul, the Lord Jesus, who appeared to you on the road as you came here, has sent me so that you may see again and be filled with the Holy Spirit'. Immediately something like scales fell from his eyes, and he could see again. He got up and was baptized, and after taking some food, his strength returned. For several days he was with the disciples in Damascus, and immediately he began to proclaim Jesus in the Synagogues, saying 'This man is the Son of God.'" (Acts 9:10-20)

Paul had now received his life's commission which was to be Jesus' apostle to the Gentiles of the Greek and Roman world. Filled with the Holy Spirit, Paul began to preach the Gospel in the synagogues in Damascus but soon angered some of the Jewish population who threatened to kill him as a traitor to his religion. Ananias and the other disciples spirited him out of the city hidden in a basket. In the Book of Acts, Paul then goes directly back to Jerusalem to speak with the apostles there. However, in Paul's letter to the Galatians, he says that he first went to Arabia for three years in order to pray and process all that had happened to him.

"But when the one who set me apart from birth and called me by his grace was pleased to reveal his Son in me so that I could preach him among the Gentiles, I did not go out to ask advice from any human being, nor did I go up to Jerusalem to see those who were apostles before me, but right away I departed to Arabia, and then returned to Damascus. Then after three years I went up to Jerusalem to visit Cephas and get information from him, and I stayed with him fifteen days. But I saw none of the other apostles except James the Lord's brother."
(Galatians 1:15-19)

Most scholars either believe that Paul journeyed to Mount Sinai (actual Saudi Arabia) or just went out into the Syrian Desert, the term "Arabia" often being a synonym for any desert area. If the former, perhaps Paul was following the path of Elijah who fled from the vengeance of Ahab and Jezebel after defeating and killing the 400 priests of Baal on Mount Carmel (I Kings 18-19:18). If the latter, then Paul may have been following the path of Jesus to go out into the wilderness and pray, processing all that had happened to him, and asking for guidance on how to accomplish his new mission in life. After this period of self-reflection, Paul traveled back from Damascus along the Via Maris to Jerusalem and discussed his conversion and mission with Peter (Cephas) and James, the brother of Jesus. Not surprisingly, most of the disciples did not want to have anything to do with Paul and it is only after Barnabas intervened and confirmed Paul's story of his road to Damascus conversion, that he was accepted by Peter and James as a new colleague.

TARSUS

Following his meeting with Peter and James, Paul traveled back to his home town of Tarsus (Figure 16). Assuming Paul's conversion on the road to Damascus occurred around 31-32 A.D., and he then spent three years in Arabia (ca. 34-35 A.D.), Paul would have arrived back in Tarsus around 34-35 A.D. We do not know how long Paul remained in Tarsus but it could have been as long as five to ten years. Tarsus, like Damascus, was an old, well-established city. The earliest written reference to the city is in a Canaanite tablet from about 2000 B.C. which mentions a Hittite city called "Tarsa". In around 1200 B.C., Tarsus was destroyed by the "Sea Peoples", groups of seafaring Aegean Greeks who raided the coastline from Asia Minor to Egypt. Tarsus was incorporated into the Assyrian Empire

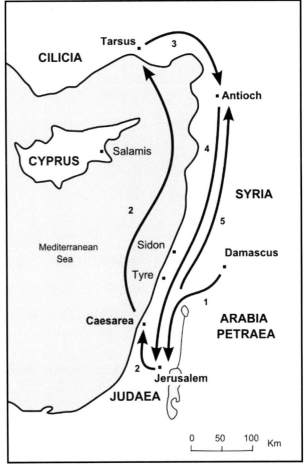

Figure 16. Map of Paul's Travels after his Conversion and his Period of Study and Ministry in Tarsus and Antioch-on-the-Orontes.
(Map Illustrated by Lance K. Trask)

in 832 B.C. but remained a relatively independent city. In 698 B.C., the Neo-Assyrian King Sennacherib sacked the city and once again Tarsus had to be rebuilt. It then passed into Babylonian control, then became part of the Persian Empire, and finally was conquered by Alexander the Great in 333 B.C. Alexander nearly died in the city after taking a bath in the frigid waters of the River Cydnus (Table 4).

Following Alexander's death in 323 B.C., Tarsus became part of the Seleucid Greek Empire and remained under Greek control until it was captured by Pompey the Great in 67 B.C. During Seleucid control, Tarsus became a major center of learning and education within the Greek world. When the Romans took control of Tarsus, the library at Tarsus reportedly contained over 200,000 "books" (actually scrolls and tablets), second only to the great library

Table 4. Key Dates and Events for Tarsus Through the First Century A.D.

Date	Event
ca. 2000 B.C.	Fortified Hittite city of "Tarsa" is recorded as one of the leading cities of the region
ca. 1200 B.C.	Destruction of Tarsus by the "Sea Peoples" (Aegean Greeks)
832 B.C.	Anatolia brought under Assyrian control but Tarsus remains an independent city
698 B.C.	Tarsus is looted by the Assyrian King Sennacherib
ca. 500 B.C.	Tarsus brought under control of the Persian Empire
333 B.C.	Alexander the Great visits Tarsus; becomes seriously ill after bathing in the cold waters of the Cydnus River
323 B.C.	Tarsus brought under the control of the Seleucids who rename it "Antioch on the Cydnus"
170 B.C.	Tarsus revolts against the Seleucids (Antiochus IV) at the same time the Jews revolt in Jerusalem
67 B.C.	Tarsus named the capital of the Roman Province of Cilicia
51-50 B.C.	Cicero serves as Proconsul of Cilicia; aggressively abolishes piracy along the coast
ca. 50 B.C.	Octavian (later Caesar Augustus) attends school in Tarsus and is tutored by the famous educator, Athenodorus
47 B.C.	Julius Caesar visits Tarsus
41 B.C.	Mark Anthony rewards the city for its loyalty to him and its opposition to Cassius; meets Cleopatra who arrives in the city via her royal barge
ca. 5 A.D.	The Apostle Paul is born as Saul to Jewish parents (Tribe of Benjamin) of Roman citizenship
ca. 18 A.D.	Paul leaves Tarsus to continue his education in Jerusalem under Gamaliel
ca. 35 A.D.	Paul returns to Tarsus from Jerusalem after his conversion on the road to Damascus (Acts 9)
ca. 40 A.D.	Barnabas goes to Tarsus and brings Paul to teach with him in Antioch (Antioch-on-the-Orontes)
44 A.D.	Cilicia reorganized under the Roman Province of Syria
ca. 47 A.D.	Paul briefly visits Tarsus after his First Missionary Journey (Acts 14)
ca 49-50 A.D..	Paul journeys through Cilicia after the Jerusalem Council and most likely stopped briefly in Tarsus

at Alexandria in Egypt. With perhaps a touch of personal pride, Paul refers to Tarsus as "no ordinary city" (Acts 21:39).

Tarsus has always been a major port and center of trade on the southern side of Asia Minor, the city being located just a few miles inland along the Cydnus River. The area is mountainous with a thin coastline. One of the few passes through the mountains to the coast, known as the Cilician Gate, is just north of Tarsus. As a result, the region had historically been plagued by chronic piracy. The Romans made Tarsus the capital of the Province of Cilicia and sent a new governor, Cicero, whose main job was to eliminate all piracy in the region and make the coastline of Asia and Palestine pirate free. Cicero declared war on the pirates of the region, the terrorists of his day, and ruthlessly eliminated them over a two year period from 51-50 B.C. According to Cicero, pirates did not deserve the courtesy of being considered formal combatants and deserved no mercy:

"For a pirate is not included in the list of lawful enemies, but is the common enemy of all; among pirates and other men there ought to be neither mutual faith nor binding oath" (Marcus Tullius Cicero)

In Cicero's day, sea travel was hazardous at best and it was the duty of all seafarers to give aid to ships in distress. Being preyed upon by pirates just added to the danger which explains Cicero's no quarter policy for pirates. In fact, many of the legal standards set out by Cicero are still the basis for International Law on Piracy today.

With the threat of piracy eliminated, trade in the region exploded and Tarsus greatly prospered under Roman rule. Octavian, later Caesar Augustus, attended school in Tarsus and was tutored by the most famous educator of his day, Athenodorus. Julius Caesar visited the city in 47 B.C. and contributed state funds for expanding the city's trade and educational centers. After his victory over the assassins of Caesar at the Battle of Philippi, Marc Anthony visited Tarsus where he met the Egyptian Queen Cleopatra for the first time.

Not much of ancient Tarsus has survived as most of the Roman city lies below 20 feet of silt and the occupational debris of modern Tarsus, the fourth largest city in Turkey with a regional population of over three million. What has been found mostly dates from the second century A.D. and includes an arch dedicated to the Emperor Septimus Severus (193-211 A.D.)

(Figure 17) and part of what may have been the Cardo Maximus of the ancient city. The street is a typical colonnaded Roman thoroughfare lined with shops; what makes it unique is that the street is paved with striking black stones made from local volcanic basalt (Figure 18).

We do not know what Paul did for the five plus years that he spent in Tarsus. However, it is likely that he practiced two occupations: (1) beginning to perfect his preaching on the word of the Gospel, probably first with the Jews and then perhaps to some Gentiles; and (2) he likely began practicing his future profession as a tentmaker. We do not know if Paul came from a family of tentmakers or he learned the profession after his conversion as a means to make a living. In the first century A.D., there were limited temporary housing establishments that today we would call hotels. Visitors to a city either would stay with friends or rent or buy a tent as temporary living quarters. A thriving port and trade center such as Tarsus would have had a continual demand for tents so it is very likely that Paul learned his profession during his stay in the city as he was established in the profession by the time he reached Corinth in 50-52 A.D. (Acts 18:3).

Figure 17. Arch to Septimus Severus in Tarsus, Turkey. (Photo Courtesy of Dr. Carl Rasmussen, www.HolyLandPhotos.org)

Figure 18. Excavated Remains of Cardo Maximus in Tarsus, Turkey. (Photo Courtesy of Dr. Cal Rasmussen, www.HolyLandPhotos.org)

During this time, the apostles in Jerusalem became aware that a number of followers of Jesus had moved to the area of Antioch in Syria in order to escape persecution by the Jewish authorities. They therefore sent Barnabas to investigate the situation and see to their ministry:

"A report about them came to the attention of the church in Jerusalem, and they sent Barnabas to Antioch. When he came and saw the grace of God, he rejoiced and encouraged them all to remain true to the Lord with devoted hearts, because he was a good man, full of the Holy Spirit and of faith, and a significant number of people were brought to the Lord. Then Barnabas departed for Tarsus to look for Saul, and when he found him, he brought him to Antioch. So for a whole year Barnabas and Saul met with the church and taught a significant number of people. Now it was in Antioch that the disciples were first called Christians." (Acts 11:22-26)

Paul departed from Tarsus and headed with Barnabas to Antioch to begin his ministry. Paul briefly visited his home at least twice more: once after his First Missionary Journey (Acts 14:28) and after he attended the Council of Jerusalem (Acts 15:23, 40-41), but neither stay was prolonged and are only hinted at by Luke in Acts.

ANTIOCH

For the next several years, Antioch became Paul's home and the church in Antioch would remain Paul's "home church" for the remainder of his life. Not only did Paul and Barnabas help found the church there but the believers in Antioch would provide prayerful support and financial aid to Paul and other Christian churches throughout the Roman world. Antioch also became Paul's sending church, for every one of his three missionary journeys began and ended at Antioch.

Antioch, or Syrian Antioch, or more correctly, Antioch-on-the-Orontes, lies in southeastern Anatolia (modern Turkey) near the Syrian border (see Figure 16). The city was founded by one of Alexander the Great's Generals and Companions, Seleucus Nicantor (359-281 B.C.). Seleucus built the city on the east side of the River Orontes at the base of Mount Silpius in 293 B.C. and named it after his father, Antiochus. Antioch was one of 16 cities built and named after Antiochus, thus there is considerable confusion when the name "Antioch" is used as to which Antioch is being referred to. This is the reason the city is often referred to as Syrian Antioch, Antioch-on-the-Orontes, or Antioch the Great (Table 5).

Antioch was originally settled by Macedonian army veterans and their families but quickly became a mixed metropolitan area with large Syrian and Jewish populations.

Table 5. Key Dates and Events for Antioch Through the First Century

Date	Event
ca. 333-293 B.C.	Alexander the Great defeats the Persian army under Darius III on the plains of Issus; after Alexander's death, one of his generals, Seleucus I, founds the city in 293 B.C. and names it after his father, Antiochus
281 B.C.	After the assassination of Seleucus I, his son, Antiochus I, transfers the capital of the Seleucid Empire to Antioch
64 B.C.	Roman General Pompey defeats Tigranes of Armenia and makes Antioch the capital of the Province of Syria
47 B.C.	Julius Caesar visits Antioch and commissions many new buildings
ca. 36 B.C.	Mark Anthony marries Cleopatra in the Temple of Apollo near Antioch
ca. 37 A.D.	Emperor Caligula sends money to rebuild Antioch after a severe earthquake destroys much of the city
ca. 43 A.D.	Emperor Claudius re-establishes Antioch's Olympic games which were to be held on a five-year basis
ca. 48-49 A.D.	Mob violence breaks out in the city during "the eighth year of Claudius"
66-70 A.D.	Period of great unrest in the city during which time a great fire breaks out which is blamed on the Jews

After Seleucus' assassination in 281 B.C., his son Antiochus I transferred the capital of the Seleucid Empire to Antioch. The city was captured by the Roman General Pompey the Great in 64 B.C. and remained a part of the Roman Empire for the next seven centuries. During the first century A.D., Antioch was the third largest city in the Roman Empire, second only to Rome and Alexandria. The city had an estimated population of over 500,000 inhabitants and was the capital of the Roman Province of Syria. The city was favored by a number of Roman Emperors including Julius Caesar, Augustus, Tiberius, Caligula and Claudius. Marc Anthony reportedly married the Egyptian Queen Cleopatra at the Temple of Apollo just outside Antioch. One of the more spectacular buildings commissioned and paid for by Augustus was the Circus (hippodrome) of Antioch. Modeled after the great hippodrome in Rome, the Circus of Antioch was 1,610 feet in length by 98 feet wide and could seat an estimated 80,000 spectators.

In 37 A.D., the city was partially destroyed by a major earthquake. The Emperor Caligula sent two senators from Rome to report on the level of destruction and then commissioned state funds to help rebuild the city. Part of this rebuilding program included a major Cardo Maximus, which was two miles in length, colonnaded and lined with thousands of shops. It is estimated that the full length of the road contained nearly 3,200 columns.

From its beginnings, Antioch had a substantial Jewish population. Being only 300 miles north of Jerusalem, the Seleucid Greeks "encouraged" Jewish rebels and their families to move north and settle in Antioch. By the first century A.D., it is estimated that Jews made up approximately 10 percent of the total city population (~50,000). Antioch was connected by a coastal road to Jerusalem and there seems to have been a close connection between events in the two cities. When Caligula attempted to place a statue of himself in the Temple in Jerusalem in 39-40 A.D., riots broke out simultaneously in both Jerusalem and Antioch. Further outbursts occurred in 48-49 A.D. when the Emperor Claudius expelled all the Jews from Rome. And lastly, when the Jewish War broke out in 66-70 A.D., there was considerable unrest in Antioch as well. Antioch served as the Roman army's gateway to the East so there was always a substantial garrison in the city with troops coming in and moving through to fight the Empire's wars on its eastern frontier. Therefore, during Paul's time in Antioch, there was always a high level of tension between the Roman occupiers and the Jews, and between the Jews and the new sect of Christian Jews.

During their initial missionary work in Antioch, Paul and Barnabas received a prophecy that a great famine was coming and would hit Jerusalem in particular:

"At that time some prophets came down from Jerusalem to Antioch. One of then, named Agabus, got up and predicted by the Spirit that a severe famine was about to come over the whole inhabited world (This took place during the reign of Claudius). So the disciples, each in accordance with his financial ability,

decided to send relief to the brothers living in Judea. They did so, sending their
financial aid to the elders by Barnabas and Saul." (Acts 11:27-30)

On returning to Jerusalem with the famine relief funds, Barnabas and Paul met with, as they described it, the "three pillars of the church": Peter, John and James, the brother of Jesus. With great enthusiasm they described their success in establishing the church in Antioch including conversion of both Jews and Gentiles to the faith. They then asked permission from these church leaders to expand the mission beyond Antioch to the rest of the Greek-speaking Roman world. Peter, John and James gave them their permission to do so, and with the addition of a young believer, John Mark, they set out for what would become Paul's First Missionary Journey.

Antioch is further featured in Paul's life through two events. The first is when Peter visited the city. At first, the Apostle willingly shared meals with the Gentile converts to the religion, but when confronted by Jewish leaders about consorting with "unclean" Gentiles, Peter restricted his meals to include only Jewish Christians. According to Paul, he confronted Peter about his hypocrisy and won the argument that all believers in Christ are of the same family (Galatians 2:11-21). Since we only have Paul's side of the story, it is unknown what Peter's reaction was to Paul's criticism.

The second event occurred after Paul's First Missionary Journey to Galatia when Jewish Christians leaders from Antioch apparently visited the region and told the new church members in Antioch Pisidia, Iconium, Lystra and Derbe that they must first become Jews before they could become Christians. This set off a long-standing dispute between Paul and the group he termed as the "Judaizers". The Judaizers were Jewish Christians that believed in order to become a Christian one had to accept three basic precepts. First, believers had to accept the seven Noahide laws: do not deny God, do not blaspheme God, do not murder, do not engage in illicit sexual relations, do not steal, do not eat from live animals, and to establish a legal system to ensure obedience to the law. Second, believers must accept the Law of Moses which included not just the 10 Commandments but all 613 of the Mitzvot of the oral and written law. Lastly, they had to accept the Covenant of Abraham, circumcision. Fundamentally, the Judaizers could not accept that God's salvation could be offered freely to anyone without having to do something in order to "earn it".

The Judaizers believed that the main Covenant between God and Man was through Abraham. Therefore in order to inherent salvation, a person needed to believe as Abraham did, which was through circumcision and the Jewish Law. Jesus' role, according to the Judaizers, was mainly to extend the Covenant of Abraham to the Gentiles.

To Paul, the beliefs of the Judaizers effectively negated God's grace. We are saved by God's grace alone, through faith alone, and not by any actions through the law because no one can keep the law perfectly. His intense belief that the Judaizers were wrong sparked two events led by Paul. The first was during the Jerusalem Council which was held in ca. 49 A.D. There, both the beliefs of the Judaizers and those of Paul were brought before the elders of the church, moderated by James as head of the church in Jerusalem. According to Paul, James and the other leaders of the church sided with him that new believers did not have to follow all the laws of Moses or become circumcised in order to become Christians. The only prohibitions they were given was that they could not eat the blood of animals and were subject to the general laws against fornication outside of marriage and worshiping idols (Acts 15; Galatians 2). The second action was Paul's "angry" letter to the Galatians in which he discussed the results of the Jerusalem Council and his dismay that the new believers throughout Galatia would even listen to the words of the Judaizers. Paul's letter to the Galatians later became the basis for Martin Luther's reformation against the Roman Catholic Church, prompted especially by the Council of Trent where the church declared that salvation could not be obtained from faith alone but needed to be combined with certain sacraments and good works.

The Judaizers had followings all across the Greco-Roman world but were particularly strong in Corinth and in Antioch-on-the-Orontes. They would continue to plague Paul's work throughout all his missionary journeys.

Very little of ancient Antioch has been exposed as it lies more than 30 feet below modern Antakya, Turkey, a thriving city of 220,000 inhabitants. A few items from the first century A.D. city have been found due to new construction, most of which are curated in the local archeology museum. The main street of Antakya (Kurtulus Caddesi) is approximately two miles in length and is situated directly above the ancient Roman Cardo Maximus.

3 GALATIA
Antioch Pisidia, Iconium, Lystra, Derbe

After receiving permission to expand their missionary work beyond Antioch and Tarsus, Paul, Barnabas and John Mark set out on what was to later be called Paul's First Missionary Journey (Acts 12:25) (Figure 19). From Antioch, the trio sailed first to Cypress arriving at the port of Salamis. Paul and Barnabas proclaimed the Gospel to the Jews in the local synagogue. They passed through the island coming to the administrative center of Paphos. There they encountered a Jewish sorcerer and false prophet named Bar-Jesus (also called Elymas). The false prophet, who was also an attendant to the regional proconsul, Sergius Paulus, attempted to turn his master against the word of the Gospel. Paul, filled with the Holy Spirit, proclaimed:

> *"You are the child of the devil and an enemy of everything that is right! You are full of all kinds of deceit and trickery. Will you never stop perverting the right ways of the Lord? Now the hand of the Lord is against you. You are going to be blind for a time, not able to see the light of the sun." (Acts 13:10-11).*

At this, Bar-Jesus was struck blind and Proconsul Sergius Paulus, who witnessed the confrontation, immediately became a believer. He was the first of many high-ranking Roman officials who became converted to the Christian Gospel. It is a common misbelief that the message from Paul and the other apostles was only received by the lowest classes in Roman society. The

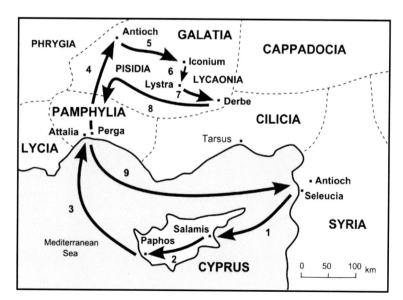

Figure 19. *Map Showing Location of Paul's First Missionary Journey. (Map Illustrated by Lance K. Trask)*

truth is that the apostles gained converts from all socio-economic levels, from slaves to proconsuls.

ANTIOCH PISIDIA

From Paphos, Paul and his companions sailed north from Cyprus to the city of Perga in the Asian Province of Pamphylia (see Figure 19). The Book of Acts is silent about whether Paul and Barnabas preached the Gospel in Perga but a major event did occur there which ultimately would cause a major rift between the two evangelists. Evidently, the two sea voyages coupled with probable hardships in traversing the island of Cyprus was too much for young John Mark. The prospect of heading further inland into the wilds of Galatia, a region that had a well-deserved reputation for bandits and dangers associated with travel, was the straw that broke the camel's back and John Mark departed for Jerusalem rather than continuing on (Acts 13:13). Much speculation has been written about who John Mark was but scholars generally agree that he was a cousin of Barnabas. Later, when Paul began his Second Missionary Journey, Barnabas again wanted to take John Mark with them. But Paul, disappointed with John Mark's desertion at Perga refused, a decision which resulted in the split between Paul and Barnabas.

From Perga, Paul and Barnabas carried on north into the Roman Province of Galatia, arriving first at the city of Antioch Pisidia. Antioch Pisidia is one of the cities founded by the Seleucid Greeks after the death of Alexander the Great and named for the father of Seleucus Nicantor, Antiochus (Table 6). The city lies on a high plain (3,260 feet elevation) which overlooks the Pisidia River and its valley. Originally settled by Macedonian army veterans, the city later became a mixture of local Lycaonians,

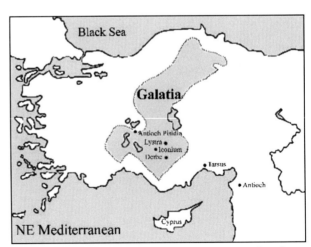

Figure 20. Map of the Roman Province of Galatia Showing Location of Major Cities.
(Map Illustrated by Lance K. Trask)

Greeks and Jews – the latter making up a sizable part of the population. Toward the end of the Seleucid Empire, Antioch Pisidia was controlled by the ruler of Pergamum, the last one of whom bequeathed the city (and the region) to Rome in his will. The Romans largely allowed the city to operate independently until 36 B.C. when Antioch Pisidia and Lystra were placed under the control of a local "client king", Amyntas. Client kings were non-Roman rulers, dependent on Rome for political, economic, and military support, and expected to serve the interests of Rome. When Amyntas died eleven years later, the region was reorganized by Caesar Augustus into the new Province of Galatia and settled by Roman army veterans (Figure 20). A total of eight Roman colonies were established in the region but only Antioch Pisidia received the formal title of Colonia Caesarea Antiochia. In 6 B.C., Augustus built the Via Sebaste, a major east-west road system linking Syria with Ephesus on the western coast of Asia Minor. Antioch Pisidia was placed at the crossroads of both the Via Sebaste and a north-south trade route, which greatly expanded the city's trade and regional importance. To protect against

Table 6. Key Dates and Events for Antioch Pisidia Through the First Century

Date	Event
ca. 300-250 B.C.	Founding of Antioch "near Pisidia" by the Seleucids
ca. 195 B.C.	Antiochus III orders the transfer of 2,000 Jewish families from Babylon to Antioch Pisidia
188 B.C.	Antioch Pisidia is declared "a free city" by the Romans
36-25 B.C.	Romans place Antioch Pisidia and Lystra under the rule of a client king, Amyntas, until his death in 25 B.C.
25 B.C.	Caesar Augustus organizes a new Roman Province of Galatia and establishes 8 colonies for settlement by Roman army veterans; Antioch Pisidia is given the title "Colonia Caesarea Antiochia"
6 B.C.	Augustus builds the "Via Sebaste" and makes Antioch Pisidia the junction of major North-South and East-West crossroads; Roman army veterans are resettled in the area to provide protection against bandits
ca. 46 A.D.	Paul and Barnabas arrive and preach in Antioch Pisidia and then move on to Iconium, Lystra and Derbe

Figure 21. Remains of the Roman Forum at Antioch Pisidia. (Photo Courtesy of Wings of Eagles Christian Tours, Brighton, Colorado)

Figure 22. Remains of the Roman Amphitheater at Antioch Pisidia. (Photo Courtesy of Dr. Carl Rasmussen, www.HolyLandPhotos.org)

Figure 23. Ruins of the Temple to the Emperor Augustus at Antioch Pisidia. (Photo Courtesy of Dr. Carl Rasmussen, www.HolyLandPhotos.org)

the threat of increased banditry, the city was settled with additional Roman army veterans who acted as a local national guard.

Augustus spent considerable funds to upgrade Antioch Pisidia, rebuilding the city along Roman urban planning guidelines with a major north-south Cardo Maximus, which intersected an east-west running Decamus Maximus. At the end of the western end of this street was the forum (Figure 21) which abutted against a large amphitheater (Figure 22). The latter dated from the Seleucid period but was upgraded twice by the Romans, once by Augustus and then later in 310 A.D. Given the amount of money that Augustus poured into the rebuilding of the city, it is not surprising that a major temple dedicated to the Cult of the Emperor was built on the eastern side of the Cardo Maximus (Figure 23). The temple itself was apparently quite small, 15 feet by 30 feet, but was framed by a much larger propylon (outer monumental gateway) and courtyard which contained statues commemorating all of Augustus' victories during his reign.

At the northern end of the Cardo Maximus was a large nymphaeum (main city water supply fountain) with a 30 foot high water tower. The nymphaeum was fed by a major aqueduct which brought 660,000 gallons of fresh water to the city every day from mountain springs seven miles to the north. This area of the city also contained a large gymnasium complex which included a public bath. Paul visited four cities in Galatia, but only Antioch Pisidia has any excavated ruins.

On their first Sabbath in the city, Paul and Barnabas entered the local synagogue and, after reading from the scriptures, were invited to speak to the congregation. This is the first sermon of Paul that is recorded in the Book of Acts (Acts 13:16-41) and shows how Paul was learning to preach the word of the Gospel. First, he started from his area of strength, Jewish scriptural history. Paul recounted Israel's history and then presented Jesus as the fulfillment of "what God promised our fathers". He then referred to John the Baptist's ministry, showing that his challenge to repent before the coming of the Messiah was also a fulfillment of scripture (Isaiah). Next, Paul introduced Jesus as the Savior and recounted how, despite his innocence, he was executed at the demands of Jerusalem's leaders and people – again as the fulfillment of prophecy. Last, Paul gave the Antiochians the news of Jesus' resurrection, which unlike the Law of Moses, makes possible the forgiveness of sins.

The sermon caused quite a stir among the congregation (Acts 13:44-52) but both Paul and Barnabas were invited back to preach on the following Sabbath. Again, the two evangelists preached the Gospel emphasizing that its message was for everyone, Jew and Gentile alike. Acts says that the whole city turned out to listen to them but the great crowds brought out the jealousy of the Jewish leaders who could not accept that God's salvation could be offered so freely to non-Jews. These leaders incited the leading men and women of the city against Paul and Barnabas and they were expelled from Antioch Pisidia. As a parting gesture, the two "shook the dust off their feet" at them (Acts 13:51) as Jesus had told his disciples to do when the word of the Gospel was rejected (Luke 9:5). Paul and Barnabas then headed east on the Via Sebaste toward Iconium (see Figure 19).

ICONIUM

Iconium lies 90 miles east of Antioch Pisidia, which would have entailed a journey of 4-5 days. Iconium was an ancient city, dating back to the beginning of the third millennium B.C. (Table 7). The city was originally controlled by the Hittite Empire but then fell under the control of a long series of invaders, starting with the Sea Peoples (ca. 1200 B.C.), then the

Phrygians (ca. 800 B.C.), the Cimmerians (690 B.C.), the Persians (539-333 B.C.), and finally the Macedonian and Seleucid Greeks. Like Antioch Pisidia, Iconium was controlled by the Kingdom of Pergamum which upon the death of its last leader, Attalos III, bequeathed the city to the Romans. The city was one of the eight colonies in Galatia that Augustus helped establish and settle with Roman army veterans and, like Antioch Pisidia, had some measure of Imperial favor. During the reign of Claudius (41-54 A.D.), the city changed its name to "Claudiconium" in honor of the Emperor.

Table 7. Key Dates and Events for Iconium Through the First

Date	Event
ca. 3000 B.C.	Area where Iconium is located was inhabited during the Copper Age
ca. 1500 B.C.	Iconium comes under control of the Hittites
ca. 1200 B.C.	Iconium comes under control of the "Sea Peoples" (Aegean Greeks)
ca. 800-700 B.C.	Area comes under control of the Phrygians
ca. 690 B.C.	Region overwhelmed by Cimmerian invaders
ca. 539-333 B.C.	Region comes under control of the Persian Empire
ca. 333-133 B.C.	Region comes under control of the Greeks (Macedonians) and later the Seleucid Empire; Iconium was ruled by the King of Pergamon; Attalos III, the last King of Pergamon, bequeathed his kingdom to the Romans on his death in 133 B.C.
ca. 41-54 A.D.	During the reign of Emperor Claudius, Iconium was re-named "Claudioiconium"
ca. 47-48 A.D.	Iconium visited by Paul and Barnabas on Paul's First Missionary Journey
ca. 50 A.D.	Paul and Silas revisit Iconium during Paul's Second Missionary Journey

Paul and Barnabas arrived in late 46 A.D. and probably spent much of the winter of 46-47 A.D. in Iconium as we are told in Acts that they spent "considerable time" in the city:

"At Iconium Paul and Barnabas went as usual into the Jewish synagogue. There they spoke so effectively that a great number of Jews and Greeks believed. But the Jews who refused to believe stirred up the other Gentiles and poisoned their minds against the brothers. So Paul and Barnabas spent considerable time there, speaking boldly for the Lord, who confirmed the message of his grace by enabling them to perform signs and wonders" (Acts 14:1-4)

However, as was the case at Antioch Pisidia, not all of those who listened to Paul's sermons came to believe in the Gospel. Acts 14 tells us that there was plot to have the two evangelists stoned but upon learning of the plot, Paul and Barnabas left Iconium and headed south to Lystra.

Ancient Iconium is completely covered by the modern Turkish city of Konya which has a population of over 1.3

Figure 24. Inscription Mentioning Iconium at the Museum of Archeology, Konya, Turkey. (Photo Courtesy of On Wings of Eagles Christian Tours, Brighton, Colorado)

million. Most of the ancient Roman city lies beneath modern Konya, but at the city center, part of the ancient acropolis is exposed as an unexcavated mound. An inscription was found in 1910 which does indicate that the mound at Konya is indeed ancient Iconium. The inscription currently resides in the small Museum of Archeology in Konya (Figure 24).

LYSTRA

Lystra lies 18 miles to the southwest of Iconium on the Via Sebaste. The history of the city is very similar to that of Iconium and Antioch Pisidia, being inherited by the Romans from the Seleucid Greeks. After a short rule by the Roman client king, Amyntas, the city was

Table 8. Key Dates and Events for Lystra Through the First Century A.D.

Date	Event
36-25 B.C.	Romans place Antioch Pisidia and Lystra under the rule of a client king, Amyntas until his death in 25 B.C.
25 B.C.	Caesar Augustus organizes a new Roman Province of Galatia and establishes 8 colonies for settlement by Roman army veterans; Lystra is populated by a mixture of Romans, Greeks and Jews
6 B.C.	Augustus builds the "Via Sebaste" and makes Lystra a Roman outpost; Lystra is garrisoned in an effort to provide protection against bandits
ca. 6 B.C. – 14 A.D.	Funded by Augustus as patron, Lystra becomes a center of education for the Province of Galatia
ca. 46 A.D.	Paul and Barnabas arrive and preach in Lystra; Paul heals a cripple and the local Lycaonians believe he is Hermes and Barnabas is Zeus (Acts 14)
ca. 48-51 A.D.	Paul revisits Lystra at least twice more (Acts 16, 18); recruits Timothy who becomes one of Paul's major disciples and co-workers

incorporated into the new Roman Province of Galatia and made a colony for settlement by Roman army veterans. When Augustus built the Via Sebaste in 6 B.C., Lystra was garrisoned in order to protect the road and the city against bandits. Funded by Augustus, Lystra became a major center of education and learning for the Province of Galatia (Table 8).

The native people of the area (referred to as incolae by the Romans) did not speak Greek but a Phrygian language called Lycaonian. Apparently neither Paul nor Barnabas understood much of the language which made communication more difficult. This language barrier played a role in a misunderstanding which occurred after Paul and Barnabas healed a lame man. Immediately a crowd gathered around the two evangelists and proclaimed that Paul must be the god Hermes and Barnabas, Zeus. This particular identification of the men with these two popular local gods may have occurred because Paul had done most of the talking (Hermes was the messenger of the gods and as such, often had a speaking role) and Barnabas may have looked much older than his companion (Zeus, as father of the gods, was always depicted as being older). The crowd wanted to sacrifice a bull in honor of the two men but Paul stopped them saying that they were only men and not gods, but they served the one who is the God of everyone (Acts 14:6-18).

In Lystra, Paul and Barnabas were truly out of their comfort zone; instead of confronting Jews in a synagogue, they were face-to-face with raw paganism. It is not known how long the

two evangelists stayed in Lystra but it appears not to have been as long as the winter stay in Iconium. Jewish leaders from both Iconium and Antioch Pisidia came to Lystra and incited the crowds against Paul. The Apostle was stoned and dragged outside the city and left for dead (Acts 14:19-20). But Paul was helped by some of the new believers from Lystra who carried him into the city and nursed him back to health. Soon thereafter, Paul and Barnabas departed from Lystra and headed east to Derbe. Paul twice referred to the event at Lystra by telling the Corinthians, "once I was stoned" (II Corinthians 11:25), and writing to the Galatians saying, "I bear on my body the marks of Jesus" (Galatians 6:17).

Figure 25. The Unexcavated Mound at Lystra, Turkey. (Photo Courtesy of Dr. Carl Rasmussen, www.HolyLandPhotos.org)

There is little to see of ancient Lystra except the mound where the unexcavated city remains (Figure 25). The city lies about a mile north of the small village of Hatunsaray. In the mid-1880's a large stone was found lying on the surface which bears the inscription "LVSTRA" identifying the site as ancient Lystra (Figure 26). In 1907, archeologist Sir William Michael Ramsey wrote "Excavation of Lystra is urgently needed in the interests of history and New Testament study". He made a second appeal for funds to excavate the city in 1941 but to no avail. To date no real work, only looting, has occurred at the site. The Lystra inscription is currently curated at the Museum of Archeology in Konya.

Figure 26. Inscription Mentioning Lystra at the Museum of Archeology, Konya, Turkey. (Photo Courtesy of Dr. Carl Rasmussen, www.HolyLandTours.org)

Paul revisited Lystra at least twice (Acts 16, 18) as part of his Second and Third Missionary Journeys. Lystra also played an important role as the birthplace of Paul's later steadfast companion and disciple, Timothy. Timothy was the child of a Greek father and a Jewish mother who became a believer in Christ. He may well have been one of Paul's early converts during his first visit to Lystra in 47 A.D. When Paul and Barnabas split company before the Second Missionary Journey over an argument about taking John Mark as their companion, it was Timothy who replaced John Mark in the role of young apprentice disciple.

DERBE

Derbe lies 60 miles to the southeast of Lystra toward the eastern end of the Via Sebaste. The city was founded around 1200 B.C. and shared a similar history to that of Lystra and Iconium. The name is believed to have come from an ancient Lycaonian word for juniper. After

Table 9. Key Dates and Events for Derbe Through the First Century A.D.

Date	Event
ca. 1200 B.C.	Derbe founded
36-25 B.C.	Romans place Antioch Pisidia, Lystra and Derbe under the rule of a client king, Amyntas until his death in 25 B.C.
25 B.C.	Caesar Augustus organizes a new Roman Province of Galatia and establishes 8 colonies for settlement by Roman army veterans; Derbe is populated by a large Jewish population
6 B.C.	Augustus builds the "Via Sebaste" and makes Derbe the last outpost on the road east towards Antioch-on-the Orontes; Derbe is garrisoned in an effort to provide protection against bandits
ca. 17 – 24 A.D.	Strabo refers to Derbe as "a Customs Station" on the Via Sebaste
ca. 41-54 A.D.	During the reign of Claudius the city receives Imperial favor as is referred to as "Claudio-Derbe"
ca. 46 A.D.	Paul and Barnabas arrive and preach in Derbe (Acts 14)
ca. 48-51 A.D.	Paul revisits Galatia (and presumably Derbe) at least twice more (Acts 16, 18)

being bequeathed to the Romans, Derbe was placed under the control of the Roman client king, Amyntas from 36-25 B.C. Following Amyntas' death, the city was incorporated by Augustus into the new Roman Province of Galatia. The city was garrisoned with Roman soldiers as the last outpost on the Via Sebaste before Tarsus and Antioch-on-the Orontes (Table 9). Like Iconium, Derbe changed its name in appreciation of Imperial favor and funding and by the mid-first century A.D., was known as "Claudio-Derbe".

The Book of Acts has but one sentence regarding the ministry of Paul and Barnabas in Derbe:

> *"They preached the gospel in that city and won a large number of disciples."*
> *(Acts 14:21)*

Afterwards, they retraced their steps, returning to Lystra, Iconium and Antioch Pisidia, strengthening the new disciples and encouraging them to be true to their new faith. They also appointed elders for them in each

Figure 27. The Mound at Ancient Derbe, Turkey. (Photo Courtesy of Dr. Carl Rasmussen, www.HolyLandPhotos.org)

of the new churches (Acts 14:21-23). Paul would return to Derbe at the start of both his Second and Third Missionary Journeys.

If there is little to see archeologically at Lystra, there has been even less to see at Derbe until very recently. The mound where the ancient city once stood is a prominent grass-covered hill which, like most Roman cities, is covered with the litter of broken bricks, stone and pottery sherds (Figure 27). In 1956, an inscription was found among the city debris which confirmed that the mound was indeed ancient Derbe (Figure 28). Like those from Iconium and Lystra, the Derbe inscription is presently curated in the Archeological Museum in Konya. In 2014, the Turkish Government initiated a small excavation on

Figure 28. Inscription Mentioning Derbe at the Museum of Archeology, Konya, Turkey. (Photo Courtesy of Wings of Eagles Christian Tours, Brighton, Colorado)

the summit of the mound at Derbe. To date, the foundations and walls of a number of buildings have been uncovered.

Figure 29. 2014 Excavations at Ancient Derbe, Turkey. (Photo Courtesy of Dr. Carl Rasmussen, www.HolyLandPhotos.org)

After going back through Antioch Pisidia, Paul and Barnabas traveled through Pamphylia and went down to the port of Attalia. From there, they took passage on a ship and sailed east back to Antioch-on-the-Orontes, completing their First Missionary Journey. At Antioch, they gathered the church together and told them of all that had been done in spreading the word of the Gospel throughout Galatia and how they had opened the door to Christianity for the Gentiles. The 14th chapter of the Book of Acts closes by saying that they "stayed there a long time with the disciples", probably from the end of 47 A.D. until early 49 A.D.

In 49 A.D., the intervention of the Judaizers led to a crisis within the new church, culminating in the Council of Jerusalem. Paul and Barnabas reported to all the gathered apostles and the elders of the church how they had opened the door to the faith to the Gentiles. Both men argued vehemently that the church should not close those doors by imposing restrictions of the Jewish faith (obedience to the law, circumcision) on the new believers. In the end, at least according to Paul, James and the other elders agreed with Paul and Barnabas that new converts to the faith did not have to first become Jews before they could become Christians (Acts 15:1-29; Galatians 2). Paul and Barnabas then returned to Antioch-on-the-Orontes to give the church the news from the Jerusalem Council and to further grow and strengthen their home church.

4 PHILLIPI

The Book of Acts says that after some time in Antioch, Paul and Barnabas decided to make another missionary trip to Asia, this time going even further westwards to the large cities along the Aegean coast. But before they left Antioch, a major rift occurred between Paul and Barnabas over the role of John Mark:

"Some time later Paul said to Barnabas, 'Let us go back and visit the believers in all the towns where we preached the word of the Lord and see how they are doing. Barnabas wanted to take John, also called Mark, with them, but Paul did not think it wise to take him, because he had deserted them in Pamphylia and had not continued with them in the work. They had such a sharp disagreement that they parted company. Barnabas took Mark and sailed for Cyprus, but Paul chose Silas and left, commended by the believers to the grace of the Lord. He went through Syria and Cilicia, strengthening the churches." (Acts 15:36-41)

The evangelists divided up the work with Barnabas taking his cousin, John Mark, and returning to his ancestral homeland of Cyprus. This is the last mention of him in Acts but he is referenced briefly in Paul's letter to the Galatians. Paul, now accompanied by Silas, went north along the landward route to his homeland of Cilicia, beginning his Second Missionary Journey (Figure 30).

Paul and Silas visited all the newly formed churches in Galatia

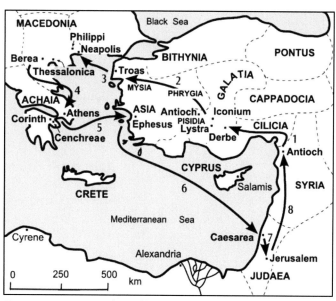

Figure 30. Map of Paul's Second Missionary Journey. (Map Illustrated by Lance K. Trask)

and they picked up Timothy in Lystra to assist them with their ministry. Paul had planned to go to the large cities of Asia along the Aegean coast (Ephesus, Sardis, Pergamum, etc.) but was prevented from doing so by the appearance of the Holy Spirit (Acts 16:6). He then wanted to head to the region of Bithynia, which included the city of Byzantium (later Constantinople, later Istanbul). But again, the Spirit of the Lord Jesus prevented him (Acts 16:7). Prevented from going west to Ephesus and east to Byzantium, Paul and his compatriots traveled the only way left to them, north to Troas and the Hellespont (see Figure 30).

It is unknown why the Holy Spirit prevented Paul from going to Ephesus or Byzantium. Perhaps it was because these two regions would later become the major evangelizing regions of John (Ephesus) and Peter (northern Galatia). In any event, Paul's movement to Troas became a watershed moment in his life, second only to his conversion along the road to Damascus. Paul now was poised to receive a new direction which would bring Christianity into Europe:

"So they passed by Mysia and went down to Troas. During the night Paul had a vision of a man of Macedonia standing and begging him, 'Come over to Macedonia and help us'. After Paul had seen the vision, we got ready at once to leave for Macedonia, concluding that God had called us to preach the gospel to them." (Acts16:8-10)

Standing in Troas, Paul and his companions could not have known that they were actually on top of nine successive cities, one of which, Troy VIIa (archeologists number successive cities at a site using Roman numerals), is likely the city of King Priam and the site of the great Trojan War of Homer's Iliad. Troas or Troy has been witness to a number of the great men of history. Xerxes passed through it on his way to invade Greece. Alexander the Great stopped in Troy to sacrifice to his childhood hero, Achilles, before conquering the Persian Empire. Here, Lysimachus, one of Alexander's Generals and Companions, built Alexandria Troas in honor of his friend. Julius Caesar passed through and eyed the city as a possible future capital. Likewise, Constantine considered Troas as a capital before settling on Byzantium. By the first century A.D., Troas was a typical Roman seaport, connected to the rest of Asia by a major road system (Figure 31) and complete with colonnaded streets, a forum, shops and a public bath (Figure 32).

Figure 31. Roman Road at Troas, Turkey. (Photo Courtesy of Leon's Message Board, www.bleon1.wordpress.com)

Figure 32. Roman Bath at Troas, Turkey. (Photo Courtesy of On Wings of Eagles Christian Tours, Brighton, Colorado)

Something else happened to Paul, Silas and Timothy at Troas which is also of significance to the story in the Book of Acts. Prior to Paul's arrival in Troas, the Book of Acts is told in the third person (Peter did this; Paul went there; they preached here). But in Acts 16:10, the narrative suddenly switches to the first person plural ("we got ready at once to leave for Macedonia"). The switch to a personal account is believed to be because the author of the Book of Acts, the Greek physician Luke, had joined the missionary team. Church tradition states that Luke was a native of Antioch-on-the-Orontes, but that is far from clear. If he was, he may have been one of Paul's converts. As a physician, he may have journeyed to the great cities along the Aegean coast or to Greece for his education in medicine. Luke may even have been practicing medicine in Macedonia and came over to Troas to get Paul to come and preach in Greece. We will likely never know the answer to this riddle but what is certain, is that Luke joined the Second Missionary Journey and then stayed with Paul for the rest of the evangelist's life.

Setting sail from Troas, Paul and his team sailed a straight course to the island of Samothrace, and from there, to the port of Neopolis. Neopolis (modern Kavala, Greece) was the port city for Philippi, located 11 miles inland (Figure 33). Little remains of the ancient city, especially from the first century A.D. The major aqueduct visible in the middle of the town today dates from the sixteenth

Figure 33. The Port of Modern Kavala (Neopolis), Greece.

century A.D. but was built on top of the original Roman structure. The only significant reference to Paul is the monument outside the Church of St. Nicholas, a few blocks north of

Figure 34. Monument to Paul at Kavala (Ancient Neopolis), Greece.

Figure 35. Stone Columns at the Monument to Paul at Kavala (Ancient Neopolis).

today's harbor (Figure 34). On one side, the monument depicts in a mosaic the dream that Paul had of a Macedonian man imploring him to come over to Greece from Troas while on the other side, Paul is depicted stepping off the boat into continental Europe. In front of the monument are the remains of three stone columns which tradition says were the pier stones which Paul tied his boat to upon his arrival in Neopolis (Figure 35).

From Neopolis, Paul and his companions headed west along the Via Egnatia. The Via Egnatia was a road that ran west to east across Greece for a distance of 686 miles connecting the Adriatic coast to Byzantium on the Black Sea. The road started at the port of Dyrrachium on the Adriatic and crossed the modern countries of Albania, the Republic of Macedonia, Greece and ended in European Turkey.

The road was constructed as a super highway of its day, connecting the colonies of northern Greece (Macedonia, Thrace) with the Adriatic and the Bosporus. With a short sea voyage across the Adriatic, the road also provided a link with Rome itself. The Via Egnatia was constructed like most major Roman roads, being built in multiple compacted layers of sand and gravel which were capped by polygonal flagstones. The road was about 20 feet in width and was built with a slight crown and major gutters on each side to allow for quick water runoff. The Via Egnatia ran through the center of Philippi and although it was an east-west road, it served as the Cardo Maximus for the city (Figures 36-37).

Figure 36. The Via Egnatia at Philippi, Greece.

Figure 37. Detail of the Via Egnatia at Philippi Showing Gutter System.

Entering Philippi from the east, the city is flanked by the Gangites River to the south and by the Pangaion Mountains to the north. The city originally was a Thracian gold mining camp known as Crenides (Spring or Well), gold having been found in veins in the Pangaion Mountains (Figure 38). To help finance his expansion of the Macedonian homeland, Philip II, the father of Alexander the Great, annexed the area in 356 B.C. Philip arranged for the region to provide him with an annual output of gold (about $1 million in today's gold values) and in exchange, he helped build a walled city which he named Philippi for himself. The Philippians were granted a degree of autonomy as long as the shipments of gold continued to be sent to Philip's capital at Pella (Table 10).

In 168 B.C., Rome defeated the Macedonians and annexed the entire region as a Roman Province. Philippi had declined in importance as the gold mines had largely played out and it was not deemed to be of any major strategic importance. This changed in 42 B.C. when Octavian (later Augustus) and Marc Anthony cornered the forces of Caesar's assassins on the plains west of the city. At the ensuing Battle of Philippi, Cassius was killed and Brutus committed suicide, effectively ending the rebellion. Although Marc Anthony engineered the victory (Octavian was ill in his tent for much of the battle), Octavian always attributed his rise to ultimately becoming Rome's first Emperor to the victory at Philippi. Accordingly, he settled it with the heroes and veterans of the XXVIII Legion and poured finances into building Philippi into "a miniature Rome".

Figure 38. Pangaion Mountains Overlooking Ancient Philippi.

Table 10. Key Dates and Events for Philippi Through the First Century A.D.

Date	Event
356 B.C.	City founded by Philip II of Macedon (Alexander the Great's father) on the site of an ancient gold mining settlements called "Crenides" (Spring or Well); Philip builds a defensive wall and grants the citizens a degree of autonomy (people of Philippi registered as Philippians and not as Macedonians)
168 B.C.	Region is conquered by the Romans; Philippi declines in importance
42 B.C.	Battle of Philippi; Octavian (later Augustus) and Mark Anthony defeat the forces of Cassius (who is killed) and Brutus (who commits suicide); city is settled and garrisoned by members of the XXVIII Legion; Octavian turns Philippi into a "miniature Rome" and it becomes the most famous city in Macedonia
31 B.C.	After Octavian's victory over Mark Anthony and Cleopatra at Actium, Philippi is renamed "Colonia Augusta Julia Philippensis" and granted Imperial Favor
ca. 50 A.D.	Paul, Silas, Timothy and Luke arrive in Macedonia and travel through Philippi; Paul meets Lydia "by the river" and forms the first Christian church in Europe; Paul is beaten and falsely imprisoned; after threatening the rulers of Philippi for illegally beating a Roman citizen, Paul is escorted out of the city (Acts 16)
ca. 55-56 A.D.	Paul travels through Macedonia and visits the church in Philippi (Acts 20)
ca. 57 A.D.	Paul, in route to Jerusalem, stops in Philippi with Luke to celebrate Passover (Acts 20)

After Octavian defeated Marc Anthony and Cleopatra at the naval Battle of Actium in 31 B.C., Philippi was renamed Colonia Augusta Julia Philippensis and was granted special privileges including a significant reduction in taxes. Philippi was, in every sense of the word, a Roman city: its language was Latin, its laws were Roman, and the money bore Latin

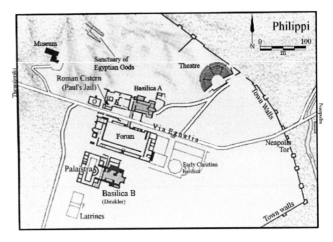

Figure 39. Map of Ancient Philippi. (Map Illustrated by Lance K. Trask)

inscriptions. Thus Paul was truly entering an alien world, a culture very different from anything he had experienced up to this date.

Because of its geographical location along the Via Egnatia, Philippi was not laid out in typical Roman fashion (Figure 39). As noted above, the east-west running Via Egnatia served as the Cardo Maximus for the city. The main Roman forum which featured a colonnaded stoa on three sides, was situated immediately south of and adjacent to the Via Egnatia. A series of north-south side roads led to the old Greek agora, a large Greek amphitheater (Figure 40), and a series of small temples to the north of the Via Egnatia in the Pangaion Mountains.

Figure 40. Large Greek Amphitheater at Philippi.

Paul, Silas, Timothy and Luke arrived in Philippi in ca. 50 A.D. By now, Paul had established an effective method of going to the local synagogue on the Sabbath where as a visiting Pharisee he would be invited to speak. He would preach the key elements of the Gospel showing how Jesus' life, death and resurrection were not only predicted by Jewish history but were the fulfillment of God's plan for all people. However, when the evangelists arrived at Philippi, they found that there was no synagogue in the city as the Jewish population was very small. Despite having no formal place to worship, the Jews that did live in Philippi met on the Sabbath at a place outside the city walls along the Gaggitas (Gangites) River:

"On the Sabbath we went outside the city gate to the river, where we expected to find a place of prayer. We sat down and began to speak to the women who had gathered there. One of those listening was a woman from the city of Thyatira named Lydia, a dealer in purple cloth. She was a worshiper of God. The Lord opened her heart to respond to Paul's message. When she and the members of her household were baptized, she invited us to her home. 'If you consider me a believer in the Lord,' she said, 'come and stay at my house'. And she persuaded us." (Acts 16:13-15)

Lydia was a dealer in purple-dyed cloth, a trade that had flourished since ancient times. The fact that no husband is ever mentioned implies that she was a widow, but unlike many widows throughout the first century A.D. Roman world, she was not destitute. On the contrary, Lydia appears to have been a prominent business woman who likely owned her business and her own house. In 1872, a Greek archeologist found a piece of white marble in Philippi which bore the following inscription: "The city honored from among the purple-dyers, an outstanding citizen, Antiochus the son of Lykus, a native of Thyatira, as a benefactor". Unfortunately, this marble inscription has since been lost but it shows that the purple cloth dyers of Thyatira may have worked in Philippi as a guild and their profession was held in high esteem.

On an interesting side note, when I visited Philippi in 2017, there were still several households located to the west of the city that maintained the purple-dyed cloth industry, mainly for the tourists. They market all sorts of dyed articles, each one labeled as "Lydian Purple". However, the color is not what we today would call true purple (violet) but instead a purple red, almost magenta color. When questioned, the people insisted this is the true color of ancient Lydian Purple.

Figure 41. The Gaggitas (Gangites) River at Philippi. This photograph was taken near the traditional site of the Apostle Paul's meeting with Lydia and her fellow believers.

In Acts 16:13-15, Luke described Lydia as a "worshiper of God". This phrase is often used to describe someone who was not Jewish by birth but later came to worship God (a proselyte). When Lydia and her household came to believe in the Lord, they not only became the first European Christians, but Lydia's house became the first European Christian church. The area along the Gaggitas (Gangites) River where Lydia's conversion to Christianity took place is now commemorat-

Figure 42. The Lydia Baptistery at Philippi.

ed with a baptismal area (Figure 41). A much larger baptistery in the name of Lydia has been built just to the north of the site (Figure 42). Tradition maintains that the location of Lydia's house was either on the site of the baptistery or on that of a nearby small hotel (Hotel Lidia).

After staying and preaching in Philippi for some time (perhaps several weeks), Paul and his companions encountered a young slave girl who, being possessed by an evil spirit, had the ability to predict the future. This girl followed Paul around shouting, "These men are servants of the Most High God, who are telling you the way to be saved" (Acts 16:17). While her message was certainly true, Paul probably did not want the Gospel to be seen coming from a

demon-possessed person. So in the name of Jesus Christ, he commanded the evil spirit to leave the girl (Acts 16:18). Unfortunately, this slave girl and her ability to see the future was the way her owners made their living and once the spirit left her body, she no longer had the ability for prophecy. Angry at losing their source of income, the owners of the slave girl brought charges against Paul and Silas before the magistrate of the city. In Roman law there was no statute that dealt with property that had been depreciated via an exorcism, so the owners of the slave girl based their charges against Paul and Silas on introducing new religious practices that had disturbed the peace of the city. Jews were not allowed to proselytize Roman citizens and it was probably on this basis that the owners' charges were based.

In most Roman cities of the first century A.D. magistrates did not have their own building but administered legal decrees from a judgment seat, or bema, usually located at a

Figure 43. The Roman Forum at Philippi. Paul and Silas were severely flogged with rods here and then thrown into jail. The area at one end of the forum marked by four steps has been suggested as a possible location of the city's bema or judgement seat.

Figure 44. Remains of Shops Lining the Roman Forum at Philippi.

prominent place on one side of the city forum. This site was often in the middle of an area of shops and when a decree or ruling was read out, the people would stop shopping and gather to listen to their city leaders. Paul and Silas were dragged through the forum to the location of the bema, where the magistrate pronounced that they should be stripped and beaten with rods (Figures 43 and 44). The jailer was given strict orders to make sure that the two foreign trouble makers would spend an uncomfortable night in jail.

While sitting that night in jail, Paul and Silas began to sing hymns to God when a violent earthquake struck the city:

"About midnight Paul and Silas were praying and singing hymns to God, and the other prisoners were listening to them. Suddenly there was such a violent earthquake that the foundations of the prison were shaken. At once all the prison doors flew open, and everyone's chains came loose. The jailer woke up, and when he saw the prison doors open, he drew his sword and was about to kill himself because he thought the prisoners had escaped. But Paul shouted, 'Don't harm yourself! We are all here'. The jailer called for lights, rushed in and fell trembling before Paul and Silas. He then brought them out and asked, 'Sirs, what must I do to be saved?' They replied, 'Believe in the Lord Jesus, and you will be saved – you and your household.' Then they spoke the word of the Lord to him and to all the others in his house. At that hour of the night the jailer took them and washed their wounds; then immediately he and all his household were baptized. The jailer brought them into his house and set a meal before them; he was filled with joy because he had come to believe in God – he and his whole household." (Acts 16:25-34)

The statement that the jailer was scared to the point of committing suicide is not an exaggeration by Luke. Roman prison laws were very harsh and typically maintained that if a prisoner escaped due to carelessness on the part of the jailer, the jailer would then take the place of the escaped criminal and carry out the remainder of the prisoner's sentence, whatever the degree of the crime. Since the magistrate had given very strict orders to the jailer before releasing them to his custody, he could be assured of being tortured at best, and executed at worst.

The traditional site for this miracle is a small building located immediately north of the forum on the north side of the Via Egnatia. When excavated by French archeologists in the early part of the twentieth century, the structure was found to be the remains of a Roman cistern (Figure 45). That does not mean that the cistern could not also have been used as a jail sometime during the life of the structure. Roman prisons often had either an outer and an inner room, or a street level room and a small, dark, subsurface room where the prisoners were kept. The cistern structure at Philippi has an outer room and an inner room that has no windows, so it certainly qualifies as to what a Roman prison cell would look like on all accounts.

The next morning, the local magistrate sent word to the jailer to release the prisoners and escort them out of the city. Paul, however, decided to turn the tables on his tormentors. He sent word to the magistrate that first, both he and Silas were Roman citizens, not Greeks, some other nationality or slaves, and secondly, as such, they had been beaten and imprisoned without trial,

Figure 45. Roman Cistern that is the Traditional Site of Paul's Prison at Philippi.

something which was against Roman law. The shoe was now on the other foot and under Roman law, the magistrates could be liable for serious penalties should higher authorities hear of their illegal actions against a pair of Roman citizens. They therefore apologized to Paul and Silas and asked them to please quietly leave the city. Having made his point, Paul first went to Lydia's house to strengthen the members of the new church in Philippi, and then left the city heading west along the Via Egnatia for Thessalonica.

Paul would maintain a strong relationship with the Philippians throughout his life. He would visit the city at least twice more: at the beginning of his Third Missionary Journey and before sailing for Jerusalem at the end of the same trip (Acts 20). Moreover, during Paul's long stay in Ephesus between 54-57 A.D., he was visited by Epaphroditus, a member of the church in Philippi. Epaphroditus brought gifts and probably sustaining funds from his friends in Philippi (Philippians 4:18). Later when Epaphroditus fell ill while in Ephesus (Philippians 2:25-30), news of his illness reached Philippi and his friends and fellow church members were very distressed. After his recovery, he returned to Philippi carrying a letter of love and encouragement from Paul which is believed to form the basis for most if not all of the Book of Philippians.

5 THESSALONICA, BEREA AND ATHENS

"Now when they had passed through Amphipolis and Apollonia, they came to Thessalonica, where there was a synagogue of the Jews."
(Acts 17:1)

Amphipolis was the capital of Macedonia Prima, which encompassed the region east of the Strymon River, to which Philippi also belonged. The city is located about 30 miles west of Philippi and lies about halfway between Philippi and Thessalonica.

THESSALONICA

The missionaries traveled on to Thessalonica, the capital of Macedonia Secunda, the second region of the Roman Province of Macedonia. Thessalonica was founded by Cassander, one of Alexander's Generals and Companions, in 315 B.C. After Alexander's death in 323 B.C., his Empire was divided amongst his generals with Cassander getting Macedonia and Greece. Cassander named the city Thessalonica after his wife, Thessalonike, half-sister to Alexander. It is believed that Cassander had a number of local villages destroyed and forcibly moved their entire populations into his new city. A major port was constructed to facilitate trade and a defensive wall was built around the city.

When Rome conquered Macedonia in 168 B.C., Thessalonica became a Roman city. In 148 B.C., Macedonia became a full Roman Province and Thessalonica was made its capital. Its key location further underscored its importance to the Romans. The Via Egnatia was initially constructed from Dyrrachium on the Adriatic coast to Thessalonica. It would later be extended further west to Neopolis through Philippi. This made Thessalonica not only a seaport on the Aegean, but the most important sea port along the main east-west road of the Roman Empire. Moreover, Thessalonica was also the port for a major north-south road that stretched from the Danube River in the north to the Aegean in the south. Octavian and Marc Anthony traveled to Thessalonica after their great victory over Cassius and Brutus at the Battle of Philippi. Grateful for the city's support in their pursuit of the assassins of Julius Caesar, Octavian made

Table 11. Key Dates and Events for Thessalonica Through the First Century

Date	Event
315 B.C.	City founded by Cassander, one of Alexander's the Great's generals and ruler of Macedon and Greece; city named for his wife, Thessalonike, half-sister to Alexander
168 B.C.	Region is conquered by the Romans
148 B.C.	Macedonia becomes a full Roman Province and Thessalonica is named its capital; the Via Egnatia is built first as far as Thessalonica and then later on to Neopolis through Philippi
ca. 50 A.D.	Paul, Silas and Timothy arrive in Macedonia and travel through Thessalonica where he preaches for three weeks; Jews from Thessalonica, angered by Paul's teachings, drive Paul out of the city (Acts 17)
ca. 55-57 A.D.	Paul travels through Macedonia and probably visited the church in Thessalonica (Acts 20)

Thessalonica a "Free City" like Athens. This meant that there were no Roman soldiers garrisoned in the city and that local government was in the control of an assembly of people, from whom magistrates (Politarchs) were chosen (Table 11).

Until the Second World War, when the Nazis rounded up and sent almost its entire Jewish population to the gas chambers, Thessalonica was known for having the largest concentration of Jews in all of Greece. However, many of these people immigrated to the city during the Inquisition when they were expelled from Spain, so we do not know for certain how large a Jewish population was present in the city during the first century A.D. The Books of Acts tells us that Paul and his companions went into the local synagogue on the first Sabbath after their arrival in the city. In strict Jewish legal terms, a synagogue (literally a "Bringing or Gathering Together") required at least 10 Jewish males in order to be built. However, given the financial cost of constructing even a modest house of worship, there was probably a considerable Jewish population in the city when Paul arrived in ca. 50 A.D.:

"As was his custom, Paul went into the synagogue, and on three Sabbath days he reasoned with them from the Scriptures, explaining and proving that the Messiah had to suffer and rise from the dead. 'This Jesus I am proclaiming to

you is the Messiah', he said. Some of the Jews were persuaded and joined Paul and Silas, as did a large number of God-fearing Greeks and quite a few prominent women. But other Jews were jealous; so they rounded up some bad characters from the marketplace, formed a mob and started a riot in the city. They rushed to Jason's house in search of Paul and Silas in order to bring them out to the crowd. But when they did not find them, they dragged Jason and some other believers before the city officials, shouting: 'These men who have caused trouble all over the world have now come here, and Jason has welcomed them into his house. They are defying Caesar's decrees, saying that there is another king, one called Jesus.' When they heard this, the crowd and the city officials were thrown into turmoil. Then they made Jason and the others post bond and let them go." (Acts 17:2-9)

The above is the only account we have about Paul's visit to Thessalonica. We see from Luke's account that Paul went into the synagogue, and using his superior background in the scriptures, laid out the three main principles of the Gospel that (1) the Old Testament prophets had spoken about a suffering Messiah (Isaiah 53; Psalm 22), (2) that after his death, the Messiah would rise again, and (3) that the crucified Jesus was the Messiah, the Christ. Paul apparently also spoke about the coming Kingdom of God as he later reminded them of this in one of his letters to the church ("Do you not remember that when I was still with you I told you this" – II Thessalonians 2:5). The fact that Paul spoke about God's Kingdom is further supported by the charges the Jews made to the leaders of the city that the evangelists had defied Caesar's decrees.

Shortly before Paul's visit to Thessalonica in around 50 A.D., the Emperor Claudius expelled the Jews from Rome for sedition, primarily based on the fact that the Christian Jews (the Romans initially made no distinction between the Jews and Christians) were proclaiming the new Kingdom of God:

"After this, Paul left Athens and went to Corinth. There he met a Jew named Aquila, a native of Pontus, who had recently come from Italy with his wife Priscilla because Claudius had ordered all the Jews to leave Rome." (Acts 18:1-2)

"Since the Jews constantly made disturbances at the instigation of Chrestus, he
[the Emperor Claudius] expelled them from Rome." (Suetonius)

The Jewish officials that were jealous of Paul and his successful ministry were using recent events to persuade the city leaders of Thessalonica to do the same to the new Christian trouble makers.

Luke's account in Acts states that the Jewish leaders rounded up some known "bad characters" that were present in the city's forum. Until 1962, there were no exposed ruins from the first century A.D. in Thessalonica because the modern city, now the second largest city in all of Greece, has been built on top of ancient Thessalonica. When an old bus station was demolished in 1962 to make room for a new city administration complex, the historic Roman forum was exposed and excavated. The city leaders decided to place the administration building elsewhere and preserve the area encompassing at least part of the forum as a permanent archeological site (Figure 46).

Figure 46. The Roman Forum at Thessalonica.

Typical of most Roman markets of the first and second century A.D., the forum perimeter at Thessalonica was lined with columns which provided shade and weather protection for the shops which also surrounded the central forum (Figure 47). Many of these shops had well-built subsurface levels which were probably constructed in order to provide cold storage for perishable items such as meat or fish or to keep wine cool (Figure 48). At one end of the forum, one of the best preserved theaters, or odeons, was uncovered (Figure 49). These small theaters were reserved for poetry recitals, intimate plays, or

Figure 47. Shops Surrounding the Roman Forum at Thessalonica.

Figure 48. Subsurface Level of Shops Surrounding the Roman Forum at Thessalonica.

music performances. Nearby, a small private bath was discovered. Guests would wash themselves in the small clay-lined pits then relax for a hot steam bath from a fire built in the center of the structure (Figure 50). Such small complexes were typically not available to the general public and were reserved for the most well-to-do citizens and city leaders. The 1962 excavations also discovered a small coin mint near the location of the odeon. Few Roman cities were authorized to mint their own coins which further emphasizes both the city's wealth and its degree of autonomy.

Paul and his companions were obviously not at the house of Jason (Acts 17:5) and in Acts 17:10 we are told that his new followers in Thessalonica

Figure 49. Roman Odeon (theater) at One End of the Forum at Thessalonica.

Figure 50. Private Roman Bath at Thessalonica.

quietly spirited him out of the city so no harm would come to them. Paul returned to Thessalonica at least once more in his life, probably on his return north through Greece to Jerusalem at the end of his Third Missionary Journey. Even though Paul did not spend much time in the city, he was able to establish a fledgling church composed of both Jews and Gentiles, although it was more heavily Gentile (I Thessalonians 1:9). Even after departing the city, he continued to be concerned about its church and the welfare of the believers. After Paul left Thessalonica, he briefly visited briefly both Berea and Athens before traveling to Corinth. During his stay in Corinth, Paul penned his first letter to the new church in Thessalonica. His concern for the new churches in Macedonia was such that instead of keeping Timothy with him in Corinth, he sent him north to Thessalonica to deliver the letter. Paul's letter, believed to be the first part of what would become New Testament scripture, is full of the type of caring one would expect from a good shepherd who is deeply concerned for the moral and spiritual welfare of his flock. This concern is reflected in his admonitions about their sexual conduct and married life (I Thessalonians 4:3-8). Paul also reassured the church that while he believed Christ's return was imminent, the absolute timing is unknown to humans as the Lord "will come like a thief in the night" (I Thessalonians 5:2).

Timothy reported that there were problems in the new churches, especially in Thessalonica. Charges had been made against Paul and he attempted to defend himself and his ministry in a second letter to the Thessalonians. Some of the new believers were being treated badly by their fellow citizens and Paul reminded them of the on-going tribulations in Judea and elsewhere against fellow Christians. Apparently some of the members of the church were so sure that Christ's return was imminent that they stopped working and were pursuing a life of spiritual contemplation. Their complete refusal to work forced others in the new Christian community to support them which had become a significant financial burden. In his second letter to the Thessalonians, Paul goes to great lengths to show that the time of the Lord's reappearance had not yet come since the "man of lawlessness" (the Antichrist) had not yet come. He admonished the idlers to go back to work saying "If anyone will not work, let him not eat" (II Thessalonians 3:10).

BEREA

After being spirited out of Thessalonica at night, Paul and his companions traveled about 50 miles southwest over a spur road that connected Thessalonica with Berea (Figure 51). Berea is located on the eastern slope of Mount Vermion and overlooks a large plain which is well-irrigated by the waters of the Haliacmon and Axius Rivers. The city was reportedly founded by and named after a legendary Greek figure named Beres about 1000 B.C. Berea (or

Beroea in ancient spellings) enjoyed a great deal of prosperity under the reign of Philip II and his son Alexander, who made it the second most important city in Macedonia after their capital, Pella. Berea reached its peak in terms of regional importance under the Antigonid dynasty of Macedonia (306-168 B.C.) when the city was made the seat of government (Koinon) for all of Macedonia. When the Romans conquered Macedonia in 168

Figure 51. Remains of the Roman Road Connecting Berea with Thessalonica.

B.C., Berea was incorporated into the new Province of Macedonia. However, its previous importance declined as the Romans favored Thessalonica and Philippi over Berea. The city then became a major center of pagan religious worship, although there appears to have been a

Table 12. Key Dates and Events for Berea Through the First Century A.D.

Date	Event
ca. 900-1000 B.C.	City founded and named for its mythical founder, Beres
ca. 356-323 B.C.	City enjoys great prosperity under both Philip II of Macedon and Alexander the Great who make it second only to their capital Pella in all of Macedonia
ca. 306-168 B.C.	Berea reaches its height of power and prosperity under the Antigonid Dynasty of Macedonia; city becomes the Seat (Koinon) of Government for Macedonia
168 B.C.	With the Roman capture of Macedonia, Berea is incorporated into the Roman Province of Macedonia; city declines in power relative to Philippi and Thessalonica under the Romans; Berea becomes a major center of worship
ca. 50 A.D.	Paul, Silas, Timothy and Luke arrive in Macedonia and travel to Berea after being driven out of Thessalonica; Paul finds the citizens of Berea much more tolerant and willing to listen to his message of the Gospel (Acts 17); however, Jews from Thessalonica come to Berea and his believers help Paul escape the city via ship to travel southwards to Athens
ca. 56-57 A.D.	Paul travels through Macedonia and probably visited the church in Berea (Acts 20)

significant Jewish population as there was at least one synagogue in the city when Paul and his companions arrived (Table 12).

As was his now established practice, Paul immediately entered the local synagogue and began to preach the Gospel of Christ:

> *"On arriving there, they went to the Jewish synagogue. Now the Berean Jews were of more noble character than those in Thessalonica, for they received the message with great eagerness and examined the Scriptures every day to see if what Paul said was true. As a result, many of them believed, as did also a number of prominent Greek women and many Greek men. But when the Jews in Thessalonica learned that Paul was preaching the word of God at Berea, some of them went there too, agitating the crowds and stirring them up. The believers immediately sent Paul to the coast, but Silas and Timothy stayed at Berea. Those who escorted Paul brought him to Athens and then left with instructions for Silas and Timothy to join him as soon as possible."* *(Acts 17:10-15)*

As would be consistent for a center of religious worship, the Bereans not only listened to Paul's message but then studied the Scriptures for themselves to see if all the references Paul gave them were true. As a result, many came to believe that Jesus was indeed the Messiah and the fulfillment of the Scriptures. Moreover, as was the case in Philippi, a number of prominent women also came to believe. This underscores two things which occurred over and over again throughout Paul's ministry. First, the word of the Gospel was received by people from all levels of society, not just the lowly as is sometimes portrayed today. Second, the message had a particularly strong appeal to women. In the first century A.D., with a few exceptions, women across the Roman world were largely treated as second class citizens with few rights and privileges outside the home. The Christian message of equality for all people, regardless of rank, race, or gender, had a strong appeal to many who felt disenfranchised in the earthly Roman world. It is therefore not surprising that a large number of the early Christian church leaders were women, such as Lydia in Philippi and the Greek women in Berea.

As Paul had experienced previously in Galatia, while the people in Berea did not cause him trouble, trouble came to the Apostle from elsewhere. In this case, the angry Jews from Thessalonica, having missed their chance at "justice" in their city, received word that Paul was preaching in Berea and came to see him punished for his "blasphemy". Fearing for his life, the believers again took Paul out of the city to safety. This time they placed him in a ship bound for Athens. Paul left Timothy and Silas to continue the work in Berea while he (and probably Luke) continued on to Achaea. The fact that Silas and Timothy could stay on in Berea without fear of retribution is a clear indication that Paul had been the one who had provoked the most violent opposition to the preaching of the Gospel.

Some scholars suggest that Paul may have traveled to Athens by land rather than by ship. There is an interesting addition in some Greek Orthodox versions of Acts which says: "He neglected Thessaly, for he was prevented from preaching the word to them" (Acts 17:15 of the Western Text of Acts). This could also mean that Paul was forced to bypass Thessaly, the region south of Berea and north of Athens, because he traveled by ship from Berea down to Athens.

Figure 52. Monument to the Apostle Paul in Berea.

There is virtually nothing from the first century A.D. to be seen in modern Veria (ancient Berea). Outside of the exposed portions of the Roman road (see Figure 51), there is a large monument to Paul and his ministry near the center of town (Figure 52). The impressive white marble monument contains three mosaics depicting the Apostle Paul in the center, flanked by scenes of him receiving the message to come to Macedonia and him preaching to the Macedonians. Local tradition suggests that the monument is placed on the site of the first century synagogue but there is no archeological evidence to confirm or deny this.

It is unknown if Paul re-visited Berea during his Third Missionary Journey. If so, it may be that he stopped in Berea briefly on his return from Attica through Macedonia before taking a ship back to Jerusalem.

According to tradition, Sopater was the first convert to the new church in Berea. He is mentioned as one of Paul's helpers during his Third Missionary Journey (Acts 20:4). The Greek Orthodox church refers to a man named Karpus as being one of the Seventy Disciples – the early emissaries sent out to preach the Gospel by Christ (Luke 10:1-24) – and also as the first Bishop of Berea.

ATHENS

Sailing southward from Berea, Paul would have passed the island of Euboea and then the southern end of Attica, known as Colonna because of the white columns of the Temple of Poseidon which are still a naval landmark today. After sailing around Cape Sounion, Paul would have spotted the port of Piraeus which serves as the link to the sea for the city of Athens. The port was originally built in the fifth century B.C. and is still very active today. From Piraeus he would have clearly seen the white marble buildings of the Acropolis, with its magnificent

Figure 53. The Acropolis in Athens. (Photo Courtesy of ExxonMobil Greece)

temple to Athena gleaming in the sunlight (Figure 53).

Athens was founded around the end of the fourth millennium B.C. as a small defensive settlement on top of the Acropolis (Table 13). The city was named for the goddess Athena who was considered the patron of the city. Over the years, Athens became the leading city-state of Achaea and one of the leading cities in all Greece. In the Greek Classical Period (the fifth and fourth centuries B.C.), Athens became a center of enlightenment for all of Greece and was known for its architecture, culture and schools. With the rise of the Persian Empire, Greece became a target for Persian expansion. In preparation for the city's defense, Themistocles, the leader of Athens, commissioned the building of 200 warships for protection against foreign invasion. Even so, Darius I and his Persian army landed on the plains of Marathon in 490 B.C. just north of the city. The Athenian army, reinforced by some volunteers from the city-state of Plataea, defeated the much larger Persian army and stopped the invasion. Despite this victory, the Athenians knew that the Persians would try to conquer Athens in the future. Darius I died in 486 B.C. and it took his son, Xerxes, several years to put down revolts across the Empire

Table 13. Key Dates and Events for Athens Through the First Century A.D.

Date	Event
ca. 3000 B.C.	City founded around the end of the 4th Millennium B.C. as a small defensive settlement on top of the Acropolis; city named for the goddess Athena who was believed to be the patron for the city
ca. 594 B.C.	Solon appointed as "archon" (ruler) of the Greek city-state of Athens
493 B.C.	Themistocles builds a fleet of 200 warships to protect the city and its commerce
490 A.D.	Athenians under Themistocles defeat the Persian army under Darius I at the Battle of Marathon
480 B.C.	Athenian fleet destroys the Persian fleet under Darius's son Xerxes at the Battle of Salamis; Athens is burned by the Persian army before retreating back into Asia
461-429 B.C.	Rule of Pericles who commissions the building of the Parthenon on top of the Acropolis; the "Golden Age" of Classical Greece
399 B.C.	Death of Socrates by order of Athens' rulers
338 B.C.	Athenians defeated by the Macedonians under Philip II at the Battle of Chaeronea
168 B.C.	Athens supports Rome in its conquest of Macedonia
ca. 150 B.C.	Attalos III, King of Pergamum, in gratitude for his education in Athens, commissions the building of the great Stoa in the agora
88-86 B.C.	Athens revolts against Rome; revolt is crushed by the Roman General Sulla who destroys Athens' Long Walls
15 B.C.	Marcus Agrippa, Augustus' son-in-law, commissions the construction of the great odeon in the agora
ca. 50 A.D.	Paul visits Athens and "reasons" with the Stoics and the Epicureans on the Areopagus

before he could assemble an army to once again invade Greece. In 480 B.C., the Persians crossed the Hellespont near Troas (Troy) and entered Greece. They quickly moved down the Aegean coast until they came to a small pass between the mountains and the sea known as Thermopylae. There, a small group of 300 Spartans under the King Leonidas, along with 700 Thespians and 400 Thebans held the vast Persian army at bay for three days. In the end, the Spartans were betrayed by a local goat herder who showed the Persians a path that led behind the Spartans, enabling the Persians to trap them between two forces. After the defeat of the Spartans, Athens was evacuated. Xerxes moved down the coast and burned much of the city. However, the Athenian fleet under Themistocles caught the Persian fleet in the straights of Salamis and effectively destroyed it. Without a source of naval supply, Xerxes felt that his army could become trapped so he retreated back into Asia, ending the Second Persian War (the First War was decided at Marathon).

In the aftermath of the victory over the Persians, the Athenians rebuilt Athens. As part of this rebuilding program, two walls known as the "Long Walls", made of sun-dried mud brick on top of cut limestone foundations, were built from two ports to Athens. The western wall, about six kilometers long, connected Athens with its port Piraeus. The eastern wall, about five and one-half kilometers long, connected Athens with another port, Phaleron, leaving a large triangle of land in between which could be used for agriculture. The walls completely encircled Athens and its ports, effectively making the city an island for the purpose of defense. As long as Athens was connected to its ports and controlled the sea, no enemy could capture the city.

Following the death of Themistocles, Pericles became the leader of Athens and ushered in the "Golden Age" of the city (461-429 B.C.). In addition to completing the Long Walls defensive system, Pericles commissioned the building of the Parthenon, a

Figure 54. The Parthenon on Top of the Acropolis in Athens.

great temple to the goddess Athena, on top of the Acropolis (Figure 54). Construction began in 447 B.C. and was completed nine years later. The Parthenon was built on top of an earlier temple to Athena which had been largely destroyed by the Persians. The temple is 228 feet in length by 101 feet wide. There are 46 outside Doric columns and 23 interior columns, each 34 feet in height and 6 feet in diameter with 20 carved flutes. On the exterior of the stones forming the lintel and the side roof were dozens of exquisitely carved sculptures of the gods and goddess from the Greek pantheon. In its interior was a sanctuary to the goddess Athena which contained a 38 foot high statue of the goddess which was completely covered in gold. The entire building was made from marble quarried at Mount Pentelikon and moved stone by stone the 10 miles to Athens.

A number of other temples were also constructed on the summit of the Acropolis; the most famous, other than the Parthenon, is the Erechtheion, constructed between 421 and 406 B.C. The temple was constructed by the master mason Phidias who also was responsible for overseeing the construction of the Parthenon. Dedicated to Athena and her victory over Poseidon for control of Athens, the Erechtheion is famous for its "Porch of the Maidens", which contained six draped female figures (caryatids) as columns (Figure 55).

Figure 55. The Erechtheion on Top of the Acropolis in Athens.

In the fourth century B.C., Athenian power within Greece began to decline. While still an important city-state, upkeep of its military forces had deteriorated such that in 338 B.C., Athens was defeated by Philip II of Macedon at the Battle of Chaeronea. Athens, along with most of the rest of the Greek city-states, were placed under Macedonian rule and forced to support the Macedonian invasion of Persia. Athens refused to actively support Alexander the Great but instead of asserting its independence, the city-state began to decline in terms of importance. Athens was an early submission to Roman occupation and actively supported Rome's conquest of Macedonia in 168 B.C. During the Roman period, Athens retained some of its status as a center of education and culture, but in terms of political and economic importance, it was eclipsed by Thessalonica, Philippi and Corinth. A belated revolt against Rome in 88 B.C. was quickly crushed by the Roman General Sulla who not only secured the city but destroyed Athens' Long Walls. They were never rebuilt.

Figure 56. The Athenian Forum and the Stoa of Attalos (right) as Seen from the Acropolis.

Athens was constructed like most Greek cities of its day, with a main entrance way which led to the central market (agora) lined with shops. However, in 150 B.C., King Attalos II of Pergamum (in Asia Minor), in gratitude for the education he received in Athens, commissioned the construction of a large, ornate covered market (stoa). The Stoa of Attalos was constructed from Mount Pentelikon marble and was 377 feet long by 66 feet wide and lined with a number of Doric columns. The Stoa of Attalos was in use until the third century A.D. when it was destroyed by invading Germanic tribes from the north. In the 1950's, the Greek government rebuilt the stoa as closely as possible to its original design and it is the dominant feature in the ancient agora today (Figure 56).

Arriving in the port of Piraeus, Paul would have walked the six kilometers to the city and passed through the Dipylon or "Double Gate" to enter the forum. Passing through the gate he would have seen the temple of Demeter with statues of the goddess and her daughter. He then would have seen a statue of a mounted Poseidon hurling his trident. Beyond this, he would have seen statues of Athena, Zeus, Apollo and Hermes, all near a sanctuary to Dionysus. Nearby was the Council House of the Five Hundred with its numerous statues to various gods and goddesses. Close to the forum there was a large stone statue to Hermes and a bronze statue to Ptolemy, one of Alexander's Generals and later Pharaoh of Egypt. Everywhere Paul would have looked, there would have been statues, sanctuaries and temples to the various pagan gods.

It is unknown if Paul ever climbed the Acropolis to look at the great Parthenon and the Erechtheion. Assuming he did, he would have entered from the south side via the Propylaea and would have passed statues of horsemen facing each other. On the right was the Temple of Athena Victory (Nike) and at the top, the Parthenon with its massive gilded statue of Athena. An ancient Greek proverb said that "there were more gods in Athens than men", and wherever the Apostle looked, on pedestals, in niches, in temples, on street corners, were gods and goddesses.

Somewhere along his way through the city, Paul discovered a statue that was labeled, "To an Unknown God". Similar statues were known throughout Greece that either paid homage to "the Gods of Asia" or "to the Unknown and Strange Gods". The purpose of these small shrines was to ensure that no deity, no matter how small or foreign, was omitted. This is not dissimilar from the Roman Catholic All Saints Day, which honors all the martyrs through history whose names are not specifically honored during the course of the year.

Paul, having been raised in the strict tradition of "You shall have no other gods before me; You shall not make for yourself a graven image, or any likeness of anything that is in heaven" (Exodus 20:3-4), would have been appalled at the degree of the pagan idolatry. But he seized upon the Athenians' own beliefs as a way of introducing God and the Gospel to them:

> *"While Paul was waiting for them in Athens, he was greatly distressed to see that the city was full of idols. So he reasoned in the synagogue with both Jews and God-fearing Greeks, as well as in the marketplace day by day with those who happened to be there. A group of Epicurean and Stoic philosophers began to debate with him. Some of them asked, 'What is this babbler trying to say?' Others remarked, 'He seems to be advocating foreign gods'. They said this because Paul was preaching the good news about Jesus and the resurrection."* (Acts 17:16-18)

As was his custom, Paul first found the Jewish synagogue and began to preach the Gospel to both the Jews and the "God-fearing Greeks", non-Jews who had become believers in God and monotheism. However, Paul also preached outside of the synagogue in the forum. There, he encountered members of both the Stoics and the Epicureans. Stoicism had been founded in Athens in the third century B.C. by the Greek philosopher, Zeno. The school of Stoicism believed that the path for happiness in life was to be found in accepting that which had been given to us and not allowing our lives to be controlled by a desire for pleasure or a fear of pain. The Stoics argued that people should use their minds to understand the world around them and their role in nature, and by working together, treat others in a fair and equitable manner.

The Epicureans were also followers of a philosophy that originated from the third century B.C. which believed that the greatest good in life should be obtained through pleasure – good food, good drink, and good companionship. Epicureanism believed that the best way to attain ultimate pleasure in life was to live modestly, gain knowledge on the workings of the world, and to limit one's material desires. In so doing, a person would attain a state of tranquility (ataraxia) and freedom from fear as well as bodily pain (aponia). The combination of these two states, tranquility and freedom from fear and pain, would then accentuate the simple pleasures of life, creating ultimate happiness.

Paul was probably not unfamiliar with both schools of thought, as there were prominent members of both the Stoic and Epicurean belief systems in his native Tarsus. Both groups enjoyed spending the day having philosophical arguments on life and the best way to live it. Paul's Jewish education, especially under Gamaliel in Jerusalem, was focused on the best way to teach the Scriptures using a series of logical arguments. Clearly, the Stoics and the Epicureans encountered in Paul someone who was every bit their equal in terms of logic and rhetoric. In their initial encounter, they referred to Paul as a spermologos, literally a "seed picker" or "babbler"; in other words, he was someone who would hang around the forum and pick up some odd words and spout them back without understanding their meaning. However, they did not totally dismiss his words because they then asked him to come before the Areopagus:

> *"Then they took him and brought him to a meeting of the Areopagus, where they said to him, 'May we know what this new teaching is that you are presenting? You are bringing some strange ideas to our ears, and we would like to know what they mean.' (All the Athenians and the foreigners who lived there spent their time doing nothing but talking about and listening to the latest ideas.) Paul then stood up in the meeting of the Areopagus and said: 'People of Athens! I see that in every way you are very religious. For as I walked around*

and looked carefully at your objects of worship, I even found an altar with this inscription: TO AN UNKNOWN GOD. So you are ignorant of the very thing you worship – and this is what I am going to proclaim to you. The God who made the world and everything in it is the Lord of heaven and earth and does not live in temples built by human hands. And he is not served by human hands, as if he needed anything. Rather, he himself gives everyone life and breath and everything else. From one man he made all the nations, that they should inhabit the whole earth; and he marked out their appointed times in history and the boundaries of their lands. God did this so that they would seek him and perhaps reach out for him and find him, though he is not far away from any of us. 'For in him we live and move and have our being.' As some of your poets have said, 'We are his offspring.'

'Therefore since we are God's offspring, we should not think that the divine being is like gold or silver or stone – an image made by human design and skill. In the past God overlooked such ignorance, but now he commands all people everywhere to repent. For he has set a day when he will judge the world with justice by the man he has appointed. He has given proof of this to everyone by raising him from the dead.'

When they heard about the resurrection of the dead, some of them sneered, but others said, 'We want to hear you again on this subject.' At that, Paul left the Council. Some of the people became followers of Paul and believed. Among them was Dionysius, a member of the Areopagus, also a woman named Damaris, and a number of others." (Acts 17:19-34)

Figure 57. The Areopagus (Mars Hill) as Seen From the Parthenon.

The Areopagus, or "Mars Hill", is a large limestone rock outcrop located between the Acropolis and the forum (Figure 57). Greek tradition stated that the Council of the Areopagus had been founded by the goddess Athena herself. By

Figure 58. Base of the Areopagus. The bronze plaque on the right commemorates Paul's speech to the Council.

the first century A.D., the Council had authority over all matters pertaining to the religious life of the city of Athens. Paul was not accused of any misdeed when he was summoned to the Council; they merely wanted to hear more about these new ideas that he had been espousing in the forum. Paul's speech, in Greek, is preserved on a bronze plaque at the base of the hill today (Figure 58).

Most Biblical scholars consider Paul's mission to Athens as a failure because he did not establish a church there, at least not on the same scale as elsewhere in Greece. Some of the listeners to his speech on the Areopagus treated Paul with contempt, others were intrigued by what they heard, and a few became followers. Of the latter, only two are named: a woman named Damaris and a member of the Council named Dionysius. Of Damaris we know nothing else. She could have been an Athenian, a Greek from somewhere outside of Athens, or even a foreigner. However, the fact that she is named probably indicates she was a person of some education and standing as common people seldom came to the Areopagus to listen to intellectual religious arguments.

As for Dionysius, the fact that Paul converted a member of the Council should be considered of some note. Tradition has it that Dionysius later became the first Bishop of Athens and was martyred during the persecutions of the Christians by the Emperor Domitian in the last decade of the first century A.D.

Paul's failure, if it can be called that, was probably not on the subject of the sovereignty of the one true God, but on the subject of Jesus' resurrection. Ever since the fifth century B.C. when the playwright Aeschylus wrote a play dealing with the subject of death, it had been a common part of Greek religious thought that there could be no such thing as a resurrection, no returning to life after death. Immortality of the soul could be possible, but the physical resurrection of the body was not only ridiculous but completely out of consideration.

With the door to more converts apparently closed, Paul moved on to Corinth. We have no record that Paul ever returned to Athens, although he lived for almost two years in nearby

6 CORINTH

There is no indication that Paul was driven out of Athens, either by a mob of angry Jews or Gentiles, or by the authorities. He simply left because he felt the prospects of gaining additional followers were slim and Corinth, with its large Jewish population, offered better ground for possible converts. Corinth was the capital of the Roman Province of Achaea and had direct communications with both the western (Rome) and eastern parts of the Empire. Moreover, while Jews lived throughout Achaea, the largest Jewish community was in Corinth. Scholars estimate as many as 20,000 Jews lived and worked in Corinth as well as throughout the Isthmus of Corinth.

CENCHREAE

Paul would have left Athens and walked to the port of Piraeus where he would have booked passage on a ship heading south to Corinth. The 60 mile journey would have taken a day and Paul's ship would have docked in Cenchreae, one of the two ports that serviced the city of Corinth (Figures 59 and 60). Corinth may or may not have been on Paul's original list of missionary destinations, but it certainly was on God's list for Paul to work there.

Figure 59. Ruins of the Port of Cenchreae.

Figure 60. Submerged Ruins of the Port of Cenchreae.

Cenchreae served as Corinth's port on the Aegean side of the isthmus. Its location was due to a deep natural harbor, the fertile plain surrounding it, and an abundance of oolitic

Figure 61. Temple of Poseidon at Cenchreae.

limestone which made an excellent building stone. The port's name seems to come from the ancient Greek word for millet, referring to the area's capacity for agricultural production. As Poseidon was the Greek god of the sea, there are a number of temples to Poseidon in the area, including one at the harbor front which would have greeted seafarers as they safely made port (Figure 61).

Southern Greece, known as the Peloponnese or Achaea, is separated from mainland Greece by a narrow isthmus that separates the Saronic Gulf on the east (Aegean Sea) from the Gulf of Corinth on the west (Adriatic Sea). The land bridge between these two bodies of waters is only 4 miles wide. The city of Corinth was in the middle of this four mile isthmus where it could control all east-west traffic. The reason the isthmus was so important to sea trade is that the waters on the southern end of the Peloponnese were notorious for high winds and violent storms. The Roman historian, Strabo, wrote "If they sail past the tip of Greece twice, they ought to forget their homes". Crossing the isthmus at Corinth not only saved time but lives and potentially lost cargo as well.

Since the establishment of Corinth in ca. 700 B.C., the area's leaders had been looking for a way to construct a canal through the isthmus in order to directly connect the Aegean and Adriatic Seas. Periander, the first great ruler of Corinth (627-587 B.C.), was the first to attempt to dig a canal but efforts quickly failed. Periander was followed by the Macedonian King Demetrius Poliorcetes, then Julius Caesar (shortly before his assassination), and then the Emperors Caligula and Nero. Vespasian, then a general in Judea, sent 6,000 Jewish prisoners to dig the canal but work stopped when Nero committed suicide in 68 A.D. and the Jewish prisoners revolted against the hard work. A canal

Figure 62. Modern Canal at Corinth.

was not finished until the Greek government completed one in 1893 (Figure 62).

Figure 63. The Diolkos Road at Corinth.

Figure 64. The Diolkos Road Showing Cart Ruts in the Limestone.

Since digging a canal proved to be impossible, Periander ordered the construction of a paved road across the isthmus in ca. 600 B.C. The road was known as the Diolkos, taken from the Greek verb dielko, meaning "to haul across". The road started near Cenchreae and then proceeded for about 5.3 miles to Lechaion, Corinth's other port on the Adriatic side of the isthmus, following the local geography so as to maintain a low gradient. The width of the roadway varied from 11-20 feet (Figure 63).

In the middle of the road, two parallel grooves were cut about 63 inches apart. In between the grooves, a wooden trackway was laid, serving as a sort of railroad. Carts or sledges would haul ship cargoes from one side of the isthmus to the other on top of the trackway. The cargo would then be loaded onto another ship and continue the voyage west. Sometimes, if the ships were small enough, the entire vessel could be transported across the isthmus. In the sense that cargoes were transported via a trackway for the trip, the Diolkos did in effect constitute a railroad – a concept that would not appear in Western Europe until about 1800 A.D. Even its gauge of about 63 inches is similar to modern standards. The worn ruts for the trackway can still be seen in some places along the Diolkos today (Figure 64).

CORINTH

Corinth is located where it is for a number of reasons. First, is its location at the isthmus between the Peloponnese and mainland Greece. This is not only a prime location for east-west sea trade as discussed above, but is also the terminus for a major north-south trade route that linked Corinth with northern Thrace and everything in between. Thus Corinth became a major

Figure 65. The Acrocorinth.

Figure 66. View of Corinth from the Summit of the Acrocorinth.

Figure 68. Ruins of the Temple of Aphrodite.

regional center for trade. In addition, the location gave rise to several significant industries including burnished bronze ("Corinthian Bronze") and fine pottery – both of which were prized all across the ancient world.

Second, the location of the city was adjacent to a large rocky promontory known as the Acrocorinth. The Acrocorinth rises 1,887 feet above the surrounding plain and provides an extremely defensible position against any potential threat (Figure 65). Moreover, the mountain has a number of fresh water springs which could supply critical water supplies for a substantial population during a siege. Therefore, even with the city located at the base of the mountain, in times of attack the entire population could be moved to an almost impregnable position (Figure 66).

The location, especially the Acrocorinth, had historical significance for a number of Greek deities and, as a consequence, for their worshipers. Corinth was the reputed home of King Sisyphus, the man who was punished by the gods for his conceit and self-aggrandizement to continually roll a large boulder up a hill only to see it roll back again once he reached the summit. It was also the home to Bellerophon, the Greek hero whose famous winged horse,

Figure 67. Bust of Aphrodite, Acropolis Museum, Athens.

Pegasus, became the city symbol for Corinth. Jason and Medea reportedly settled in Corinth after his adventure of capturing the Golden Fleece. Corinth also had significance for Zeus, Apollo, Demeter, Poseidon, Fortuna and a number of other gods and goddesses. But it was especially sacred for the goddess Aphrodite (Figure 67). A small temple was built to the goddess near the summit of the Acrocorinth (Figure 68).

Although the temple itself is relatively small (52 x 33 feet), it was renowned for being extremely wealthy, largely due to the income brought in by the over 1,000 sacred prostitutes that worked for the goddess. In 20 A.D. the Greek historian, Strabo, wrote:

> *"The Sanctuary of Aphrodite was so wealthy that it possessed as slaves of the temple more than a thousand prostitutes, who were dedicated to the goddess both by men and women. And so by reason of them, the city was thronged and enriched for the sailors spent their money easily, and on that account the proverb says: 'Not for every man is the voyage to Corinth'."*

Figure 69. Votive Offerings Recovered from the Acrocorinth, Corinth Museum.

Figure 70. Votive Offerings Recovered from the Acrocorinth, Corinth Museum.

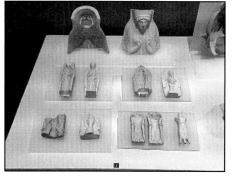

Figure 71. Molds Used to Make Idols to Aphrodite.

Excavations of the Acrocorinth by the American School for Classical Studies recovered a large number of votive offerings to the goddess including many clay figurines (Figure 69) and clay representations of wine-soaked cakes (Figure 70). Apparently there was a substantial industry in the city of Corinth which manufactured these votive figures as a number of molds for making Aphrodite idols have

Table 14. Key Dates and Events for Corinth Through the First Century A.D.

Date	Event
ca. 5000 B.C.	Area initially inhabited by farmers migrating from the Middle East
ca. 700 B.C.	City founded with a rich history in Greek mythology; reported the home of Sisyphus; Bellerophon (whose winged horse Pegasus becomes the city symbol); Jason and Medea reportedly settle in Corinth after his adventures to capture the "Golden Fleece"
627-587 B.C.	Rule by Periander; first attempt to dig a canal across the Isthmus of Corinth
ca. 600 B.C.	The "Diolkos" road is constructed
ca. 550 B.C.	The great Temple to Apollo is constructed
ca. 480-350 B.C.	Corinth becomes renowned for its fine pottery and burnished bronze ("Corinthian Bronze")
ca. 400 B.C.	"Corinthianize" becomes a byword across the entire Greek world for sexual immorality; city is well known for its large number of prostitutes and taverns
338 B.C.	Philip II of Macedon places Corinth as head of the "Corinthian League"
146 B.C.	Romans under Lucius Mummius destroy Corinth
44 B.C.	City is rebuilt by Julius Caesar; Corinth becomes the most important city of commerce in Greece
27 B.C.	Corinth becomes the capital of the Roman Province of Achaea
ca. 40 A.D.	Emperor Caligula considers building the Corinthian Canal but Egyptian engineers fear the project will flood the city of Corinth so the project is abandoned
ca. 50-52 A.D.	Paul visits Corinth and stays for 18 months; he is brought before the Roman Proconsul Lucius Gallio for sedition but the case is dismissed without a trial
ca. 57 A.D.	After several prior visits, Paul returns to Corinth for three months where he is believed to have written the Epistle of Romans
67 A.D.	Emperor Nero decides to build the Corinthian Canal; Vespasian sends 6,000 Jewish captives from Galilee to work on the project but the attempt is abandoned after Nero's death in 68 A.D.

been recovered (Figure 71). Due to the strength of the Cult of Aphrodite and its numerous prostitutes, the word "Corinthianize" became a by-word throughout the Greek world for sexual immorality. Plato, in his Republic, states that "to keep a Corinthian girl is bad for a man's health". To be called a "Corinthian girl" was not a compliment!

An oligarchy, consisting of a council of 80, began to control Corinth starting in ca. 585 B.C. (Table 14). Worried over war with rival city-state Argos, Corinth became an ally of Sparta. Later, the city leaders grew fearful of Sparta's rising power and began to side with Athens. Corinth fought with Athens against the Persian invasion led by Xerxes in 480 B.C. as it threatened not only Athens but the economy of Corinth as well.

During the Peloponnesian Wars (431-404 B.C.), Corinth first sided with Sparta against Athens and then later formed an alliance with Athens along with Argos, Boeotia and Thebes to fight Sparta (Corinthian Wars 395-386 B.C.). All of these conflicts cost Corinth greatly and the city began to decline in wealth and status.

In 338 B.C., Corinth sided with Athens against Philip II of Macedon and was defeated at the Battle of Chaeronea. Philip II, now Captain-General of all Greece, made Corinth the head of the Corinthian League, a council of Greek city-states which sent elected delegates to vote on all matters of foreign policy, under the strong guidance of Macedonia. An unfortunate consequence of this dubious honor was the stationing of a large Macedonian garrison on the Acrocorinth, effectively making Corinth a Macedonian colony. A succession of Hellenistic (Macedonian) kings controlled the city for the next two centuries.

Corinth remained a free city-state in the Achaean League until Rome set its sights on incorporating Archaea into its Republic. In 146 B.C., Corinth tried to revolt against Rome and its takeover of the region. Lucius Mummius was elected Consul of Achaea and quickly crushed the revolt. All of the men of Corinth not killed in battle were put to the sword, and the women and children of the city were sold into slavery. All the statues, friezes and works of art were seized and shipped to Rome. Corinth was then reduced to ashes. The city lay largely abandoned for a century until it was rebuilt by Julius Caesar in 44 B.C. Because of its key location, the new Corinth quickly grew in prominence and prosperity. Corinth became the capital of the Province of Achaea in 27 B.C. and by the first century A.D., the city had an estimated population of over 300,000 inhabitants.

The distance from the port of Cenchreae to the city of Corinth is about 6 miles and would have taken Paul a few hours to walk. Passing through the Cenchreae Gate, Paul would have entered Corinth from the south. What confronted him could not have been more of a contrast to his last sojourn in Athens. Where Athens was refined and a center of philosophy,

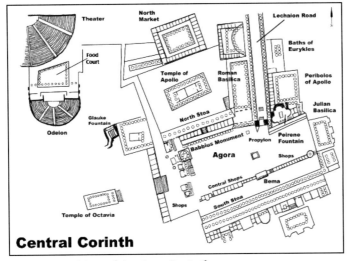

Figure 72. Map of Ancient Corinth.
(Map Illustrated by Lance K. Trask)

Figure 73. The Lechaion Road
(Cardo Maximus) at Corinth.

education and art, Corinth was vulgar and commercial. Shops and temples to various gods and goddesses were everywhere. When the Romans rebuilt Corinth in the latter half of the first century B.C., they laid the city out in the standard Roman Cartesian grid system (Figure 72). Two main roads entered the city, the Cenchreaen Road from the southeast and the Lechaion Road from the north. As the Lechaion Road was the principal north-south road into the city, it

Figure 74. The Lechaion Road Showing
Shops Lining the Road. Acrocorinth in the
background.

Figure 75. Detail of Shops Lining the Lechaion Road.

was designated as the Cardo Maximus (Figure 73) and was lined with a large number of shops (Figures 74-75). The average width of the Lechaion road, including sidewalks, was about 50

Figure 76. The Baths of Eurykles (Spring of Peirene).

feet. To the east and west of the Cardo Maximus were 12 decumani (east-west streets), 6 on the north side of the forum and 6 on the south side.

First and foremost, Corinth was a seafaring town with hundreds if not thousands of sailors arriving daily. These men had been at sea for weeks to months under fairly Spartan conditions. Merchant ships during the first century A.D. typically did not have room to provide the crew with living quarters in the

way merchants ships do today. Instead, the crew slept below in the hold where they could find space among the cargo or on the deck in warm weather. Sanitary conditions were virtually non-existent with seamen relieving themselves over the side of the ship and hoping the waves would wash the filth away. When they arrived at Cenchreae or Lechaion, they wanted to visit

Corinth and enjoy the pleasures of its many taverns, eateries and prostitutes. The city elders, on the other hand, while happy to relieve the sailors of their money, did not want the city experience to smell like a stable for its residents. So the Romans built a large public bath, the Baths of Eurykles, at the edge of the city just off the Lechaion Road and strongly encouraged visitors to bathe first before coming into the forum to shop, dine or whatever (Figure 76).

Figure 77. The Temple to Apollo at Corinth.

As Paul entered Corinth, he immediately would have become aware of all the temples and shrines to various gods and goddesses that lined the central part of the city. Towering above all was the massive Temple of Apollo. From pottery sherds left by the masons who built the temple, the structure has been dated to about 550 B.C. It was built to replace an earlier temple to Apollo which dated from the previous century. The temple was built in typical Doric style and is 174 feet long by 70 feet wide. There were 15 massive columns on each side and 6 at each end (only 7 of the original columns remain today) (Figure 77). Each column was monolithic, made from a single piece of limestone with a basal diameter of 5 feet 8 inches. A surface of white stucco marble was applied to the column in order to present a brilliant white color in sunlight. One interesting feature of the temple is that the floor beneath each massive column was slightly raised in a convex curve. This architectural feature would later be used for the columns of the Parthenon in Athens. The inner building was divided into two rooms placed back-to-back. Each room was entered by a porch which had two columns in front of them. Inside the rooms were rows of smaller columns. According to the Greek geographer Pausanius, there was a bronze statue of Apollo inside one of the central rooms.

Figure 78. Temple to Octavia at Corinth.

Walking around the city, Paul would have seen statues of the Asian Artemis (see Chapter 7), Dionysus, Zeus, Apollo, Poseidon, Aphrodite, Kthonios (of the underworld) and Athena. On the western side of the forum there were temples to Tyche (Fortuna), Heracles, Poseidon, Apollo and Hermes, as well as two precincts dedicated to the Egyptian goddess, Isis. The Cult of the Emperor was also present as above the forum on its western side was a temple to Octavia, deified sister of the Emperor Augustus (Figure 78). Outside the city was a major shrine to Apollo's son, Asclepius, the god of healing. People from all over Achaea and Greece came to this shrine to pray for healing, leaving votive clay replicas of the body part that needed healing at the shrine. Many of these can be seen today in the museum at ancient Corinth.

At the center of the city was the forum. The forum at Corinth was unusually large, being almost 500 feet in length by nearly 160 feet in width. The forum had originally been planned to be a jugerum in size (double of a square actus or about 240 Roman feet by 120 feet), but by the first century A.D., the forum was almost twice this size (Figures 79-80). On three sides, the forum was lined with a large number of shops and taverns. Most of the shops were double story structures with a ground level shop for merchandise and a smaller upper story where either the shop owners or their slaves slept and watched over the shop after closing hours (Figure 81). On the western side of the forum, archeologists investigating the "long stoa" have found a row of 33 shops, each of which has a storeroom in the rear and a well (Figure 82). The well was likely used for the cold storage of perishable goods. On a door jam in the area archeologists found an inscription in Greek which read "Lucius the Butcher" leading to the conclusion that this area of

Figure 79. Roman Forum at Corinth.

Figure 80. Roman Forum at Corinth.

Figure 81. Shops Lining the Forum at Corinth.

Figure 82. Shops Along the Long Stoa Lining the Forum at Corinth.

the forum was most likely the macellum or meat market. Other specialty product areas have also been found including a major area of shops near the western wall of the city which was the area of pottery production.

A short distance from the forum to the northwest of the city was the Roman theater, or odeon. The odeon at Corinth is a typical Roman theater with a semi-circular *cavea* (auditorium) that had seating for about 3,000 spectators (Figure 83). The cavea was cut out of the natural slope of the ground and had both a lower and upper section. Only the lower section remains today. To the north of the odeon was the larger amphitheater. It too was cut out of the natural slope of the hillside (Figure 84). Originally built toward the end of the fourth century B.C., the

Figure 83. Roman Odeon at Corinth.

Figure 84. Remains of the Greek Amphitheater Corinth.

amphitheater at Corinth had a long and complex history with numerous remodelings. By the end of the first century A.D., the amphitheater hosted gladiatorial games, complete with wild animals.

In between the two structures, archeologists found a quadrangle that contained a large number of inward facing shops (Figure 85). Inside the shops were copious amounts of pottery including significant numbers of sherds of fine dinner ware known as "Samian Ware" or Terra Sigillata. In addition to the pottery, there were large amounts of animal bones, primarily rib bones from pigs as well as bones from chickens and other food animals. Given the location of these shops in between the two theaters, archeologists concluded that the area must represent the one of world's first "fast food courts" which offered quick and easy to eat meals for the theater patrons. When the author visited the area in the spring of 2017, the ground was still littered with sherds of

Figure 85. Remains of an Apparent "Food Court" Located Between the Theaters.

Terra Sigillata ware and there was even a pig rib bone in front of one of the small shops (Figure 86).

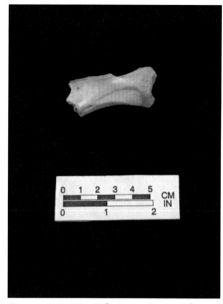

Figure 86. Pig Rib Bone Found by the Author in the Food Court Area.

The total dimensions of first century A.D. Corinth were 7,430 feet (2,265 meters) east-west by 3,484 feet (1,062 meters) north-south. The area encompassed by this was 2.4 square kilometers, or 240 hectares (593 acres) – just a little smaller than a square mile (640 acres).

Chapter 18 of the Book of Acts tells us that when Paul arrived in Corinth, he met a Jewish couple, Aquila and Priscilla, who had recently been forced to leave Rome when the Emperor Claudius expelled the Jews in ca. 48-49 A.D. This fits with the timing of Paul arriving in Corinth from Athens in ca. 50 A.D.:

"After this, Paul left Athens and went to Corinth. There he met a Jew named Aquila, a native of Pontus, who had recently come from Italy with his wife Priscilla, because Claudius had ordered all the Jews to leave Rome. Paul went to see them, and because he was a tentmaker as they were, he stayed and worked with them. Every Sabbath he reasoned in the synagogue, trying to persuade Jews and Greeks." (Acts 18:1-4)

Pontus, the home of Aquila, was the region on the southern side of the Black Sea, east of Byzantium (Istanbul). He had traveled all the way to Rome to conduct business and then back to Corinth when his Roman business was forcibly shut down by the Emperor's decree. These facts show how widespread the Jewish business population was during the first century A.D. Acts 18:1-4 also shows that Paul was conducting his tentmaking business as a means of earning a living while preaching the Gospel in the local synagogue on the Sabbath. We do not know where Paul's business was located but he, Aquila and Priscilla may have rented a space in one of the shops that lined the two main roads (Lechaion, Cenchreae) that entered the city.

When Silas and Timothy arrived from Berea, Paul was able to quit his day job and focus all his efforts on preaching:

> *"When Silas and Timothy came from Macedonia, Paul devoted himself exclusively to preaching, testifying to the Jews that Jesus was the Messiah. But when they opposed Paul and became abusive, he shook out his clothes in protest and said to them, 'Your blood be on your own heads! I am innocent of it. From now on I will go to the Gentiles.*
>
> *Then Paul left the synagogue and went next door to the house of Titius Justus, a worshiper of God. Crispus, the synagogue leader, and his entire household believed in the Lord; and many of the Corinthians who heard Paul believed and were baptized." (Acts 18:5-8)*

Note that only when the opposition to Paul's teaching became abusive (verbally? physically?) did Paul stop preaching in the synagogue. As he and Silas had done in Antioch Pisidia, Paul shook out his clothes (symbolically shaking the dust off at his detractors) and declared that henceforth he would only preach to the Gentiles (Greeks and Romans). However, Paul's message had not been in vain as the leader of the synagogue, a man named Crispus, became a convert to Jesus.

Clearly, the abuse that Paul took from his own people took its toll. To encourage him, the Lord sent him a vision:

> *"One night the Lord spoke to Paul in a vision: 'Do not be afraid; keep on speaking, do not be silent. For I am with you, and no one is going to attack and harm you, because I have many people in this city'. So Paul stayed in Corinth for a year and a half, teaching them the word of God." (Acts 18:9-10)*

Paul remained in Corinth for 18 months, which would translate to the years ca. 50-52 A.D. While he no longer went into the synagogue to preach, that does not mean that Jews from the synagogue who disagreed with the Gospel of Jesus quietly sat by without confrontation. In fact,

Acts 18 tells us that they tried to bring charges against Paul to the local magistrate, the Proconsul of Achaea, Lucius Junius Gallio:

"While Gallio was proconsul of Achia, the Jews of Corinth made a united attack on Paul and brought him to the place of judgment. 'This man,' they charged, 'is persuading people to worship God in ways contrary to the law'."

"Just as Paul was about to speak, Gallio said to them, 'If you Jews were making a complaint about some misdemeanor or serious crime, it would be reasonable for me to listen to you. But since it involves questions about words and names and your own law – settle the matter yourselves. I will not be a judge of such things.' So he drove them off. Then the crowd there turned on Sosthenes the synagogue leader and beat him in front of the proconsul; and Gallio showed no concern whatever." (Acts 18:12-17)

In an attempt reminiscent of those aimed against Paul in Antioch Pisidia, Philippi and Thessalonica, the Jews who opposed Paul's teaching tried to bring charges, probably of sedition, against him before the Roman authorities. In this case, instead of invoking a charge against Roman law or loyalty to Caesar, the Jewish charges were apparently that the Gospel of Jesus was different from what was taught in the oral and written Torah. Gallio, the Proconsul for all of Achaea, quickly saw that the case had nothing to do with Roman law and as such, dismissed it without ever seriously listening to the charges.

The narrative of Paul's time in Corinth mentions several locations and people which have been shown by archeology to have existed exactly when, where and how Luke presented them in Acts. First of all, Acts 18 mentions that on multiple occasions, Paul, as was his custom, went into the local synagogue on the Sabbath in order to preach.

Figure 87. Synagogue Inscription Found on the Lechaion Road.

Jewish custom was that visiting Rabbis and Pharisees would be asked to read from the scriptures and then afterwards, be invited to speak on a particular subject. Paul used these opportunities to preach the Gospel and show how Jesus was indeed the Messiah and the fulfillment of prophecy. So, was there a synagogue in Corinth?

We know from Roman sources that the estimated Jewish population of the city was approximately 20,000 – clearly more than enough to warrant at least one (if not more) synagogue. In 1898, archeologists found a stone on the Lechaion Road which bore an inscription in Greek, "Synagogue of the Hebrews" (Figure 87). The stone appears to be from a door lintel and while it probably dates from the fifth century A.D. based on the script used, we know that Jewish synagogues were invariably built on top of pre-existing synagogue sites. The location of the main synagogue in Corinth was most likely somewhere along the Lechaion Road. Today, at the northern end of the archeological site, there is a site where the ruins of shops along the road have stopped, leaving an open place with the remains of massive stone foundations. Many scholars believe that this was the location of the Jewish synagogue as it is only a few yards away from where the inscribed lintel stone was found (Figure 88).

Figure 88. Presumed Location of the Main Jewish Synagogue at Corinth.

Figure 89. The Bema (Judgment Seat) as Seen from the Forum.

Figure 90. Close-Up of the Bema in the Forum at Corinth.

Figure 91. Sign for the Bema in the Forum at Corinth.

Acts 18 then mentions that the Jews brought Paul "to the place of judgment" to appear before the local magistrate. As discussed in Chapter 4, the typical place of judgment in a Roman city was the "bema". In ancient Greece, the bema was simply a raised platform used by orators. Many Hebrew synagogues had a similar structure known as the bimah from which Rabbis would read the scriptures to the congregation. In the first century A.D., the bema, or more correctly the "Bema Seat" was a raised platform from which magistrates would make both civic pronouncements as well as listen to civil cases and pronounce judgments. The Romans usually placed such platforms along one side of the city forum so that crowds doing their shopping might hear the pronouncements and then pass the information on to their fellow citizens. In Corinth, the bema is a very prominent raised platform that is located in the center of the south side of the forum (Figure 89-91).

Acts 18 further tells us that the local magistrate who heard the case against the Apostle Paul was none other than the Proconsul for all of Achaea, Lucius Junius Gallio. Gallio was the brother of the famous Roman philosopher, Seneca, who was the tutor of the future Emperor Nero. In 1905, several fragments of a large stone inscription were found 120 miles northwest of Corinth in Delphi, the site of the famous Oracle. Since then, several more fragments have been found, both of the original inscription and a stone column which relates to the inscription. The inscription is part of a letter from the Emperor Claudius to the people of Delphi and reads:

"Tiberius Claudius Caesar Augustus Germanicus, pontifex maximus, in the 12th year of his tribunal power, acclaimed Emperor for the 26th time . . . sends greetings to the city of Delphi . . . but with regard to the present stories and those disputes of the citizens of which a report has been made by Lucius Junius Gallio, my friend and proconsul of Achaia . . ."

A second inscription on a stone column, also mentions Gallio as Proconsul of Achaea (Figures 92-93). The twelfth tribunal year of the Emperor extended from January 25th, 52 A.D. to January 24th, 53 A.D. From Roman sources, we know that the 23rd to the 27th acclamations of Claudius as Emperor occurred between January 25th, 51 A.D. and August 1st, 52 A.D. These acclamations typically occurred after a significant military victory by the Emperor or one of his

Figure 92. The Gallio Inscription at Delphi.

Figure 93. Close-Up Showing the Name of Proconsul Gallio.

officers. Scholars believe the 26th acclamation, the one mentioned in the above inscription, occurred sometime in the first half of the year 52 A.D. As the Gallio inscription implies that he had been Proconsul of the region for some time, Gallio probably received his appointment in 51 A.D. and his term extended through 52 A.D. We know that the Apostle Paul arrived in Corinth sometime during the year 50 A.D. and was there for 18 months. So the Gallio inscription, which confirms the man's presence in the region in exactly the office stated by Luke, fits precisely with the timeline of Paul's first visit to the city.

Lastly, a Corinthian citizen, identified as Erastus, is mentioned three times in the New Testament:

"And having sent into Macedonia two of his helpers, Timothy and Erastus, he himself stayed in Asia for a while" (Acts 19:22)

"Gaius, who is host to me and to the whole church, greets you. Erastus, the city treasurer, and our brother Quartus, greet you." (Romans 16:23)

"Erastus remained in Corinth, and I left Trophimus, who was ill, at Miletus."
(II Timothy 4:20)

These versus tell us that Erastus was no ordinary citizen of Corinth, but the City Treasurer, a man of great importance and status. In 1929, a stone inscription was found on a piece of pavement located between the two theaters at Corinth which said:

ERASTVS PRO AED SP STRAVIT

That is, "Erastus Pro Aedilitate Sua Pecunia Stravit" or "Erastus in return for his aedilship

Figure 94. The Erastus Inscription Located Near the "Food Court" Area.

laid the pavement at his own expense" (Figure 94). A Roman aedilis was equal to what we would call the City Treasurer. In the first century A.D., especially for a city the size and wealth of Corinth, this would have been a very significant position. The name Erastus was an unusual name in the first century A.D. The odds that there were two men, with the same unusual name, both of whom had the unique position mentioned by Paul in Romans, defy belief. So in the 17 short verses of Acts 18 (plus a verse from Romans and Timothy), it is awe inspiring that so many locations, features and names dealing with Paul's time in Corinth have been verified by archeology.

ISTHMIA

When the historian Strabo stated that Corinth was a wealthy city, he was not simply referring to the taxes it charged on transported goods or to the income generated by the city's many taverns and prostitutes. Corinth also controlled a small city located about 8 miles to the east named Isthmia. Isthmia is located about four miles north of the Port of Cenchreae on the Aegean Sea. The city was founded in ca. 582 B.C. and soon thereafter, a Panhellenic festival known as the Isthmian Games was established. The games were held every two years in honor of the god Poseidon. The games attracted not only the top athletes from across Greece, but many visitors and merchants. With no hotels as such in the area, most of these visitors would have wanted to rent or purchase tents, so the Isthmian Games were a huge boon to those in the tentmaking business. When the games took place, an "Isthmian Truce" was put in place between Corinth and all the other Greek city-states until the games were completed.

The Isthmian Games were held in either April or May of 51 A.D. and it is almost certain that the apostles Paul, Silas, Timothy, Luke, Aquila, Priscilla and perhaps Crispus, Erastus and other converts as well attended the games. Paul would have found the huge throngs of sports spectators a potential rich field for not only his tentmaking business but for new converts to the Gospel as well.

The Greek geographer Pausanius wrote that upon entering the sanctuary of the temple of Poseidon in Isthmia, there were "on one side statues of the athletes who had been victorious in the Isthmian Games and on the other side a row of pine trees". Archeologists from the American School of Classical Studies have found what they believe was the office of the director of the Isthmian Games. The floor of the room is adorned with a well-preserved mosaic which depicts a victorious athlete on one side holding a palm branch in his hand and wearing a wreath of leaves. On the other side is the goddess of good fortune, Eutychia, who is receiving the athlete's thanks for his victory. The Isthmian Crown given to victorious athletes was not made from fresh leaves but withered leaves of wild celery. This separated the Isthmian games from those held at Olympia and Pythia which bestowed wreathes of wild olive and laurel leaves, respectively. The fact that the wreath was made from withered leaves may have been the reason Paul referred to it as a "perishable crown" in his later letter to the Corinthians:

"Do you not know that in a race all the runners compete, but only one receives the prize? So run that you may obtain it. Every athlete exercises self-control in all things. They do it to receive a perishable wreath, but we an imperishable. Well, I do not run aimlessly, I do not box as one beating the air; but I pommel my body and subdue it, lest after preaching to others I myself should be disqualified." (I Corinthians 9:24-27)

Anyone living in Corinth during the first century A.D. would not only have been well aware of Isthmian Games but of all the events held there as well. Paul used sports metaphors frequently ("I have fought the good fight", "I have finished the race") – all of which would have had meaning to his Corinthian audience.

Figure 95. The Temple of Poseidon at Isthmia.

At Isthmia, archeologists have uncovered the foundations of the large temple of Poseidon (Figure 95). The temple was originally built at the time of the city's founding but was destroyed and rebuilt several times. The latest rebuild was after 44 B.C. when Julius Caesar gave extensive funds to have Corinth and the surrounding area rebuilt. The foundation is approximately 131 feet by 46 feet wide with a number of large columns enclosing an altar to the god inside. The temple was surrounded by a courtyard which was enclosed by a portico on three sides.

Figure 96. The Starting Gate at Isthmia.

All that has survived of the stadium in which the Isthmian Games were held is a section of the triangular starting point of the race track, which was paved with limestone slabs. The starting point was an isosceles triangle with the starter located at the apex. Grooves were cut into the starting gate to demark each runner's lane (Figures 96-97). The gate consisted of a series of vertical poles which held horizontal bars connected to the starter by a series of cords. The cords fitted within the grooves of the pavement

Figure 97. Detail of the Race Starting Gate at Isthmia.

and ran back to the starter. As he pulled on the cords, the horizontal bars across each lane fell and the race began.

Excavations at Isthmia have also uncovered what is believed to have been the finishing point of the races. The races of the Isthmian Games, like our modern Olympics, included many distances but the race of races was the straight dash. At Isthmia, the dash was 181.15 meters (594 feet). This varied slightly from the other great athletic sites where the main sprint was 192.27 meters (Olympia), 178 meters (Delphi) or 184.96 meters (Panathenian).

Paul stayed and worked in Corinth and its environs for 18 months. Then sometime either late in 51 or early 52 A.D., he left and crossed the Aegean Sea to Ephesus in Roman Asia (modern Turkey):

> *"Paul stayed on in Corinth for some time. Then he left the brothers and sisters and sailed for Syria, accompanied by Priscilla and Aquila. Before he sailed, he had his hair cut off at Cenchreae because of a vow he had taken. They arrived at Ephesus, where Paul left Priscilla and Aquila." (Acts 18:18-19)*

It was a Jewish tradition to maintain Nazirite laws during a vow (refraining from shaving, cutting of hair, drinking of wine, etc.). We do not know what the nature of Paul's vow was; perhaps it was giving thanks to God for keeping him safe while he was in "the lion's den" of immoral Corinth. At any rate, he left Corinth by the same route as he arrived, the port of Cenchreae where he purchased passage to Ephesus.

A little over four years later, Paul would make his second and probable final trip to Corinth (although a third visit is postulated by some scholars) when he would stay a further three months in the city. During this second trip, the Apostle would resolve some major problems in the church, rival factions eating meat sacrificed to pagan gods among other problems, and restore his name and standing in the church from attacks by the Judaizers (see Chapter 2). The period of relative peace during his second stay in Corinth also allowed Paul the time to compose and write his major Christian theological message to the church in Rome, the Book of Romans. Evidently Paul longed to sail from Corinth to Rome but first needed to take a large sum of money collected for famine relief back to Judea. In Romans 16 we learn that the letter was dictated to a Corinthian man named Tertius and then dispatched with a woman named

Phoebe who lived in Cenchreae. He also sent greetings from a number of Corinthian believers including Gaius, Quartus, Lucius, Jason, Sosipater and Erastus. But just as he and Timothy were getting ready to leave Cenchreae, they learned of a plot against Paul's life on the ship they were about to use (Acts 20:3). They were carrying a considerable sum of cash and perhaps the money, and not Paul, was the object of the plot. In any event, Paul and his companions left Cenchreae by foot and slowly retraced their footsteps from his Second Missionary Journey traveling north through Macedonia and then across to Troas and down the coast of Asia Minor.

As Paul turned his back on Corinth for the final time, it is interesting to speculate what may have been going through his mind. In many respects, he was probably glad to be leaving the city. The nearly two years he spent there had been hard ones, full of stress and tears. He had arrived full of anxiety at a city that would make Las Vegas blush. It was indeed a miracle, maybe one of the greatest in Paul's life, that he was able to establish and grow a Christian church in such a city. Now, seven years later, he was leaving, but he must have been deeply aware of how God's preserving love had kept him safe during all the intervening years.

Paul's ministry in Corinth had taught him what it takes to follow a crucified Lord: "Jesus was crucified in weakness, yet he lives by God's power; likewise we are weak in him, yet by God's power we live with him" (II Corinthians 13:4). Paul did not have an easy time in Corinth. He was beset by opposition from all sides: from the Corinthian culture to the Jewish community and even from followers within the new Christian church as well. Because of his persistence despite all the opposition, Corinth shaped Paul's ministry into a cruciform shape. Perhaps it was fitting that he would now be heading to Jerusalem and then from Jerusalem, to his own end in Christ's name.

7 EPHESUS

The latter part of Acts 18 tells us that after leaving Corinth, Paul sailed across the Aegean to Ephesus where he stayed a short time:

"Then he left the brothers and sisters and sailed for Syria, accompanied by Priscilla and Aquila. Before he sailed, he had his hair cut off at Cenchreae because of a vow he had taken. They arrived at Ephesus, where Paul left Priscilla and Aquila. He himself went into the synagogue and reasoned with the Jews. When they asked him to spend more time with them, he declined. But as he left, he promised, 'I will come back if it is God's will.' Then he set sail from Ephesus. When he landed at Caesarea, he went up to Jerusalem and greeted the church and then went down to Antioch." (Acts 18:18-22)

Paul left his new friends, business partners and fellow believers Aquila and Priscilla to carry on the mission in Ephesus while Paul returned to his home church in Antioch after a stop in Jerusalem to report to the apostles and elders there of all his success and failures in Greece. Paul would not return to Ephesus until later in ca. 54 A.D. during his Third Missionary Journey.

The city of Ephesus dates from ca. 980 B.C. when it was first settled by Ionian Greeks who explored and settled most of the Aegean islands as well as the western coast of Asia Minor (modern day Turkey) (Table 15). According to linguists, the site named "Apassas" in Hittite records transformed over time and became the name "Ephesus". The city was built as a sea port at the mouth of the River Caister within a valley separated by two elongate mountain ridges, the Bulbul Dagh to the south and the Panayir Dagh to the north. The native Ephesians believed that the city was near the birthplace of the goddess Artemis, and consequently, the area was sacred to the goddess. In fact, much of the history of ancient Ephesus is intimately tied to the worship associated with the Cult of Artemis.

Table 15. Key Dates and Events for Ephesus Through the First Century A.D.

Date	Event
ca. 980 B.C.	First settlement in the area by Ionian Greeks
ca. 560 B.C.	Croesus, King of Lydia, builds the second Temple of Artemis on the site of the original temple which was supposedly built and serviced by the Amazons
ca. 539-333 B.C.	Ephesus comes under Persian control
356 B.C.	The Temple of Artemis is destroyed by arson; Alexander the Great is born and the local legend is Artemis was attending to Alexander's birth and thus could not be present to defend her sanctuary
ca. 333 B.C.	Ephesus is liberated by Alexander the Great who offers to rebuilt the Temple of Artemis; the Ephesians refuse the offer and build the "Artemision" one of the Seven Wonders of the Ancient World
319-281 B.C.	Lysimachus, one of Alexander's generals, encloses the city inside a 6 mile wall and builds its great entrance streets
133 B.C.	Attalos III, King of Pergamum who has been controlling Ephesus, bequeaths the city in his will to Rome
ca. 51-33 B.C.	Ephesus is visited by a number of Roman leaders including Cicero (51 B.C.), Julius Caesar (48 B.C.), Brutus and Cassius (44 B.C.), and Mark Anthony and Cleopatra (41 and 33 B.C.)
29 B.C.	Ephesus becomes the capital of the Roman Province of Asia (instead of Pergamum); Strabo visits the city and writes a description of the Artemision and its temple prostitutes
ca. 51-52 A.D.	Paul visits Ephesus in route to Syria (Acts 18)
ca. 52-55 A.D.	Paul spends three years (off and on) in Ephesus; the riot with the silversmiths occurs in the great amphitheater (Acts 19)
ca. 57 A.D.	Paul meets with Ephesian elders in Miletus prior to going to Jerusalem

The first temple to the goddess Artemis was said to have been built and tended by the legendary Amazons around 700 B.C. When this first temple was destroyed in a massive flood, Croesus, the King of Lydia, had it rebuilt at his expense (after all, he was "rich as Croesus"). This second temple lasted until 356 B.C. when it was destroyed by a major earthquake which hit the entire region. Over the next few years, the Ephesians rebuilt the temple, turning it into one of the Seven Wonders of the Ancient World, the Artemision.

Ephesus came under Persian control in the sixth century B.C. when Cyrus the Great defeated the Babylonians and then expanded his empire west to the Aegean Sea. The city remained under Persian control for the next two centuries until it was liberated by Alexander the Great in 333 B.C. The Ephesians told Alexander that the great temple to Artemis had been destroyed in 356 B.C., the year Alexander was born, because the goddess was attending his birth and could not be in Ephesus to protect her own temple. Upon hearing the story, Alexander offered to help pay for the temple's rebuilding but the Ephesians politely refused and rebuilt the temple themselves (although Alexander most certainly contributed some funds). After Alexander's death, one of his Generals and Companions, Lysimachus (319-281 B.C.), enclosed the city within 6 miles of defensive walls and built the city's two main entrance ways, the Arcadian Way leading from the harbor (west) and Curetes Street leading from the east. Ephesus continued under Greek rule for the next 150 years, finally coming under the control of Attalos III, King of Pergamum. When Attalos died in 133 B.C., he had no male heirs or children so he left his kingdom, including Ephesus, to Rome. Ephesus would remain a Roman city for the next six centuries. In 29 B.C., Caesar Augustus named Ephesus as his capital for the Roman Province of Asia (modern Asia Minor) and in the first century A.D., the city's population has been estimated to have been between 200,000-250,000 inhabitants.

Due to the frequency of earthquakes which would periodically destroy large portions of the city, the Romans were able to slowly reorganize Ephesus into a partial Cartesian coordinate

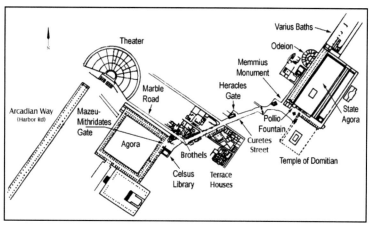

Figure 98. Map of Ancient Ephesus. (Map Illustrated by Lance K. Trask)

system (Figure 98). A particularly destructive earthquake occurred in 23 A.D. so when Paul visited the city, he would have seen the rebuilding effort from that time. There were still two main entrances to the city, one from the west via the city's harbor and one from the east on the Via Sebaste which connected the city to Syria, and all the cities of Asia Minor in between. The western approach, known as the Arcadian Way or the Harbor Road, entered through a major arch at the harbor front, was 36 feet wide and 1,732 feet long (Figure 99). The entire length was colonnaded and lined with shops. On the north side of the street near the harbor were the public baths and gymnasium complex. Visitors to the city, as was the case in Corinth, were strongly encouraged to take full advantage of the facilities before joining the rest of Ephesus' citizens in the forum, or in a restaurant or the theater. This is the way that Paul would have entered when he first arrived in Ephesus from Corinth in 52 A.D.

Figure 99. The Arcadian Way (Harbor Road) Leading into Ephesus.

On Paul's second visit to Ephesus, he traveled from Antioch along the Via Sebaste and would have entered the city from the east. From there he would have entered through the Magnesian Gate and traveled along the equally impressive thoroughfare known today as Curetes Street (Figure 100). In ancient times, this street was known as Embolos or "Wedge", as it cut diagonally across the city following the local topography (see Figure 98). This street was also colonnaded and lined with shops for much of its length. Like the Arcadian Way, large public baths (the Varius Baths) were located near the city gate to encourage visitors to bathe first before entering the heart of the city. At its upper end, Paul would have encountered the upper or State Agora, which during the first century A.D. was the administrative center of the city. Proceeding down Curetes Street, Paul would have passed the city's odeon, and then by a large altar dedicated to both Artemis and the Emperor Augustus. By placing an Augusteum in the same precinct as the altar to Artemis, the Emperor effectively made himself a partner with the goddess who was the patron deity of the city.

The next building Paul would have encountered was the emotional centerpiece of the city and the heart of Augustus' building program despite its relatively modest size. Called the *Prytaneion* (Presidents), it housed the communal hearth for the city. The goddess Hestia was symbolized by an eternal flame that burned there. The center of Greek family life was the hearth, and Hestia as guardian of the hearth symbolized happiness in the home, personal security and the sacred duty of hospitality.

Figure 100. Curetes Street Leading into Ephesus from the East.

Moving west from the Prytaneion, Curetes Street goes steeply downhill, losing 65 feet vertically for the remainder of its 700 foot length (see figure 100). The street varies from 22-33 feet in width at this point, not including the sidewalks on either side which add another 11-15 feet in width. On the southern side of the street, a series of exquisite houses were built into the hillside. Known as the

Figure 101. Frescos and Mosaics in one of the Terrace Houses, Ephesus.

Figure 102. Detail of a Mosaic from a Terrace House in Ephesus.

Figure 103. Indoor-Plumbing Clay Sewage Pipe, Terrace House, Ephesus.

Figure 104. Marble Street, the Cardo Maximus of Ephesus.

"Terrace Houses", several of these have recently been excavated and have been found to be some of the most complete and richest houses found to date across the Roman Empire. Most have multiple levels and the walls are decorated with beautiful painted frescos and many of the floors have mosaic scenes (Figures 101 and 102). The houses even have indoor plumbing, private toilets and baths (Figure 103). Clearly this area represented the living area of the wealthiest citizens of Ephesus.

Both the Arcadian Way and Curetes Street intersect a central north-south road, Marble Street, which serves as the Cardo Maxi-

mus of the city (Figure 104). Named for the glisten-
ing white marble slabs which served as the
pavement, Marble Street was colonnaded and lined
with a large number of shops (Figure 105). This
section of the city was the "Rodeo Drive" of Ephesus and shops in this area were expensive to rent or
own and carried a wide variety of luxury goods
from all over the Roman Empire. Many of the
shops had the initials of the owner carved on the

Figure 105. Shops Lining Marble Street.

pavement in front of the store. One owner, identified by the
Greek letters Theta Epsilon, must have been one of the wealthier
citizens of the city as his initials are in front of an entire row of
shops in this prime real estate area (Figure 106).

Near the center of Marble Street was the Roman forum.
The forum at Ephesus is unique, and is known as the Tetragonos
Agora, (Square Marketplace). Originally build by Lysimachus in
the third century B.C., the forum is exactly 367 feet (112 meters)
on each side (Figure 107). The forum at Ephesus was lined with
shops on all sides and had special gates which allowed entrance
to the market area. The most impressive of these was the Gate of

Figure 106. Store Owner's
Initials Carved into Marble
Street.

Mazaeus and Mithridates which was located near
the Library of Celsus on the forum's south side. All
of the shops were multi-story structures, with the
main shop area at street level and an upper living /
storage area. The entire square was colonnaded so
that shoppers could walk around the market place
sheltered from sun or rain.

Like many Roman cities of the first century
A.D., Ephesus provided a number of public facili-

Figure 107. The Roman Forum at Ephesus.

ties for its citizens and visitors. These included several large public latrines, centrally located
near the major shopping areas. Roman latrines were rarely segregated by gender, being unisex

facilities. This was aided by the fact that both men and women typically wore long robes in public which could be hiked up when sitting on the latrine while still maintaining privacy. Seats were laid out in a rectangular fashion (Figure 108). In front of the patron was a small trough that contained running water. Each seat was provided with a stick to which a sponge was affixed. The sponge served as toilet paper and each patron was obliged to clean it in the water trough for the next user before leaving. Sewage was deposited in a sewer system which carried the waste away, usually to the nearest river, or in the case of Ephesus, to the ocean.

Other public facilities included the great library

Figure 108. Public Latrine Adjacent to the Forum.

of Celsus (Figure 109). Paul would have seen a more modest facility as the great library was not constructed until the first quarter of the second century A.D. It was built in honor of the Roman Senator Tiberius Julius Celsus Polemaeanus by his son, Gaius Julius Aquila (Consol). Today, its multi-story reconstructed façade is one of the centerpieces of ancient Ephesus. The building is believed to have housed between 12,000-15,000 scrolls making it one of the largest libraries in Asia. It also served as a mausoleum for Celsus who is buried in a crypt beneath the library in a decorated marble sarcophagus. There was also an auditorium attached to the building where lectures on various subjects were given. However, not everything that went on in the library was purely academic. When archeologists excavated the library, they discovered a secret tunnel underneath

Figure 109. The Library of Celsus.

Figure 110. Remains of Brothels Near Intersection of Curetes and Marble Streets.

Figure 111. Inscription in Pavement of Marble Street Giving Directions to Brothel.

Marble Street that led from the library to a complex of buildings on the other side of the street. These buildings had signs which clearly indicated what they had been used for – brothels (Figure 110)! In fact, in the pavement along Marble Street, there is a sign which gives directions to this brothel complex. The sign has a prominent left foot, a portrayal of a female pubic triangle, and a picture of a woman's head. Beneath the head is a small square with some writing. One of the interpretations of this advertisement is "Turn left at the crossroads and buy the love of a woman" (Figure 111). Ephesus, like Corinth, was a sea port and prostitution was both legal and big business.

At the end of Marble Street, near its intersection with the Arcadian Way, is the great amphitheater. It was originally believed that this structure had been built by Lysimachus (ca. 319-281 B.C.) but current opinion is that no theater existed prior to the first century B.C. The amphitheater may have been built to celebrate Ephesus' incorporation into the Roman Empire. The structure is built into the hillside of Panayir Dagh

Figure 112. The Roman Amphitheater at Ephesus.

Figure 113. Roman Amphitheater at Ephesus. The three sections can clearly be seen separated by two horizontal diazomata.

and is easily seen when entering the city via the Arcadian Way (Figure 112). The amphitheater is the sixth largest in Asia and has a seating capacity of 25,000-30,000. The cavea (seating area) has 66 rows of seats, divided by two diazomata, (walkways between the seats) into three horizontal sections (Figure 113). In the lower section, many of the seats had marble backs and were reserved for the most important people. A box made exclusively for the Emperor has also been found. The audience entered from the top with women and children sitting in the uppermost section, middle class and working men in the middle section, and patricians and important visitors in the lower section.

The theater's stage was a three-storied structure that was nearly 60 feet high. The façade facing the audience was decorated with reliefs, columns with niches, windows and statues. There were five door opening onto the orchestra area, the middle one of which was wider than the rest. This enhanced the appearance of the stage, giving it a bigger, monumental look (Figure 114).

Figure 114. The Stage in the Amphitheater at Ephesus.

Immediately in front of the amphitheater and on the north side of the Arcadian Way, archeologists have found the remains of a very unusual cemetery (see Figure 112, foreground). Based on carvings on the tombstones, this cemetery appears to have been reserved for gladiators and their families. The fact that women and children have been found alongside the adult males shows that many gladiators lived long enough to marry and have families. Gladiators were expensive to buy and even more expensive to train. As a result, actual to the death matches as depicted in the movies were rare.

Ancient texts refer to gladiators taking "a drink of ashes" after matches. Historically, this has been thought to have been wood ash mixed with vinegar or sour wine but the reason for this ritual was not known. Detailed forensic analysis of the skeletal remains of the gladiators at Ephesus has shown that the bones have anomalously high concentrations of the element strontium, and that the men lived on a diet that was super-rich in carbohydrates. A high carbohydrate diet would have put on fat (think Sumo wrestlers) on top of the muscle tissue. Fat bleeds profusely when cut but protects the underlying muscle tissue. A gladiator that was made of rippling muscles with no fat would have been quickly, and perhaps permanently, disabled by sword cuts. Accordingly, with a layer of fat covering the muscles of the gladiators, the audience would have been able to see what they wanted – blood – but the fat would have preserved the gladiator's fighting strength.

Diets which are very rich in carbohy-drates tend to leach calcium from bones. Bone strength was critical for a gladiator as his armor and weapons weighed a great deal (gladiator helmets alone frequently weighed as much as 8 pounds). Wood ash is known to be high in calcium as well as strontium which travels chemically in association with calci-um. Thus a drink of wood ash mixed in vinegar would have provided a good calcium supplement to offset the negative effects of the gladiator diet.

Figure 115. Temple to the Emperor Domitian.

Ephesus was also a major center of pagan worship. Statues and small shrines to most of the Greco-Roman gods were present through-out the city. As mentioned above, Augustus attempted to insert himself into the Artemis myth, combining both the goddess cult and the Cult of the Emperor. After Paul's death, the Emperor Domitian (81-96 A.D.) not only had himself declared a living deity but had major temples to himself built throughout the Empire, including Ephesus (Figure 115). Domitian was so hated that many of these were torn down or repurposed upon his death.

Figure 116. Carved Monument to the Goddess Nike (Victory).

Everywhere Paul would have turned there would have been carved images of various pagan gods (Figure 116). But the worship of these other gods was not as prominent in Ephesus as the cult to the goddess Artemis. To truly understand what Paul was fighting against in

Ephesus and over much of Asia Minor, one has to understand the origins and beliefs inherent in the Cult of Artemis.

THE ASIA MINOR CULT OF ARTEMIS (DIANA)

The Greeks are well known to have worshiped a large pantheon of gods and goddesses. The Romans adopted many of the Greek gods, usually giving them Roman names: Zeus became Jupiter, Hermes became Mercury, Poseidon became Neptune and so forth. One of these Greek deities was Artemis, who in Rome became known as Diana. As Rome expanded its territorial reach through the first century A.D., the Romans also adopted a number of foreign deities that were worshiped elsewhere in the Empire (outside of Greece and Rome). Two of the more prominent of these foreign deities were Isis from Egypt and the Asia Minor cult of Artemis (Diana).

Figure 117. Statue of the Greek Goddess Artemis in the Vatican Museum showing her as she was originally depicted in Greek mythology as the Goddess of the Hunt.

Artemis was originally the Greek goddess of the hunt, forestry and hills, and archery. Later, she also became associated as the goddess of the moon. According to Greek mythology, Artemis was the daughter of Zeus and Leto, a Titan goddess whom Zeus found irresistible and subsequently impregnated. Leto bore twins, Artemis and her brother Apollo. Artemis was born first and, according to mythology, seeing that her mother was exhausted from childbirth, she assisted in the birth of her brother Apollo the following day. From this act, Artemis also became known as a protector of mothers and childbirth. Greek legends tell of Artemis growing up in the woods, hunting with her bow and frequently accompanied by deer or hunting dogs (which became her sacred animals) as well as young virgin maiden companions (Figure 117). Artemis later appealed to Zeus to forever maintain her virginity, which he granted. She was pursued by many suitors but always remained the perpetual virgin.

Somewhere along the line of the Artemis myth, she also became the goddess of the

Figure 118. Statue of the Greek Goddess Artemis in the Vatican Museum showing her as the Goddess of the Hunt with the Crescent Moon as part of her Headdress.

moon. As such, she is also commonly depicted with a crescent moon either above her head, in her head-dress, or at her feet (Figure 118). Never a major deity in Greek life, there were specific temples to her in Attica and on Crete.

By approximately 550 B.C., the Greek goddess of Artemis had morphed into an all-together different mother goddess figure in Asia, although not in Greece, at least at first. There had always been a strong mother goddess cult in Asia, including Mesopotamia, Asia Minor and Palestine. Frequently, this goddess figure was the consort of the principal male god. As civilization became more sedentary and more dependent on cereal grain harvests, both the primary male god and his consort became fertility figures with the female goddess also taking on the role as protector of women, the home and childbirth. This goddess figure was known by a number of names: Inanna or Ishtar in Mesopotamia, Astarte-Anath-Asherah in Palestine and the Levant, Ma in eastern Asia Minor, and Cybele in Phrygia and southern Asia Minor.

With the rise and subsequent fall of the Persian Empire, many of those nations that once made up Mesopotamia, Asia Minor and the Levant lost their physical, if not cultural, identity. Moreover, there was a focused effort by the Greeks after the death of Alexander the Great to "Hellenize" Asia, including the introduction of Greek culture, language and religion. Somewhere between the end of the Assyrian and Neo-Babylonian Empires and the advent of Hellenization across Asia, the original Greek goddess Artemis changed identity, losing the goddess of the hunt persona and adopting the role of an overall mother goddess. As such, Artemis also became the protector of women, fertility and childbirth. As many of the Middle

Eastern fertility goddesses were already associated with the moon, this characteristic was retained along with Artemis' perpetual virginity. Depictions of the new mother goddess Artemis from this era show her as a rigid figure encased in a tapering cylinder from above the waist to the feet. She wears a crown which is often designed like city walls. Heads of bulls and rams flank her face and the lower half of her body. She is festooned with a number of egg-shaped objects across her chest which have variously been identified as female breasts, eggs, or even the testicles of bulls (Figure 119). All vestiges of the maiden goddess of the hunt are gone. When Rome conquered Asia Minor in the second and first centuries B.C., the Asian Artemis was given the Roman equivalent name, Diana, and she was worshiped thereafter in the eastern part of the Empire as either Artemis or Diana.

The change in Artemis' character from goddess of the hunt to mother goddess necessitated a change in her background story as well. The Asian Artemis was believed to have been born in the woods near the city of Ephesus in southwestern Asia Minor. She retained the filial relationship to Apollo but the story of her

Figure 119. Artemis as Asia Minor Mother Goddess from a Statue in the Vatican Museum. The egg-shaped objects lining the figure's chest have been variously identified as female breasts, eggs or bull's testicles – all symbols associated with fertility.

assisting her mother in his birth as midwife was magnified. Her birth in the region was further associated with the fall of an object from the heavens, probably a meteorite, which was said to bear the image of the goddess.

The great temple to the Asian Artemis was built in Ephesus sometime in the latter part of the fourth century B.C. Known as the Artemision, it was 450 feet in length by 225 feet in width. One hundred and twenty seven ornately carved columns, all made

Figure 120. Remains of the Temple of Artemis at Ephesus Today. (Photo Courtesy of Chris Friedersdorf)

from the finest white marble, held up its 60 foot high roof. At its center was a worship area which contained a large statue to Artemis and the smaller image of Artemis that was said to have fallen from the sky. Iron meteorites can be polished to a mirror-like finish and properly placed, could have reflected sunlight in an impressive manner. The Artemision lasted for over 700 years, finally being destroyed in a great earthquake in 401 A.D. Stones from the temple were taken for other structures and the temple was never rebuilt due to the spread of Christianity over the region. Today, almost nothing remains of the great Temple of Artemis (Figure 120).

Figure 121. Bronze coin from First Century A.D. Ephesus showing bee symbol. (Wilson W. Crook, III Collection)

The head of the cult of Artemis at Ephesus was a chief priest, usually a eunuch, who carried the title Megabyzos (possibly meaning "set free by god"). Other attendant priests were referred to as Essenes and were usually prominent local towns-people who served for a term of one year. So many priestesses served in the temple at Ephesus that they were referred to as *melissai* (bees). Ancient records indicate there were at least three classes of priestesses but we no longer know what the duties of each class were. However, their importance is unquestioned as the city symbol for Ephesus became a bee (Figure 121).

Figure 122. Marble idol of Artemis from Ephesus. (Wilson W. Crook, III Collection)

Temple prostitution, especially alongside the pathway leading up to the temple, was prolific. Worship of Artemis, as with many Asian fertility deities, was a sympathetic or syncretic religion. The worshipers acted out, in concert with the priests and priestesses, the role they wished the gods to play in order to promote fertility in heaven and on earth. As Ephesus was located along the major east-west and north-south crossroads of trade for the eastern part of the Roman Empire, great wealth poured into both the city and the temple. Many of the religious pilgrims carried with them currency from all over Asia and as a result, Ephesus, and the Temple of Artemis in particular, became great centers of currency exchange as well. This further increased the wealth of the city and the temple.

As is the case with souvenir-seeking tourists today, many visitors to the Temple of Artemis wished to purchase a figure of the deity to take home with them. As a result, a large business sprang up in the manufacturing of images of the goddess from clay, ivory and precious metals (Figure 122). These manufacturers of Artemis idols along with the cult worshipers of the goddess became some of the most ardent opponents to the Apostle Paul in his ministry in Ephesus and throughout Asia Minor. The Book of Acts records this conflict between Paul and the idol makers in Ephesus in which they confront the Apostle shouting "Great is Artemis of the Ephesians".

Ephesus was not the only city in Asia Minor where the worship of Artemis flourished. Many of the other cities of the Roman Province of Asia (Asia Minor) had temples dedicated to the goddess as did the cities of the Decapolis in the Middle East, now primarily modern day Jordan. The worship of the Asian Artemis even spread back to Greece, notably in Philippi where there was a large cult to the goddess. At Jerash, north of Amman in Jordan, where Artemis was the patron goddess as she was in Ephesus, there was a major temple to the goddess situated on a hill overlooking the city. The temple was completed in about 150 A.D. and was ornately decorated with fine marble paneling and a decorated cult statue within the main worship area.

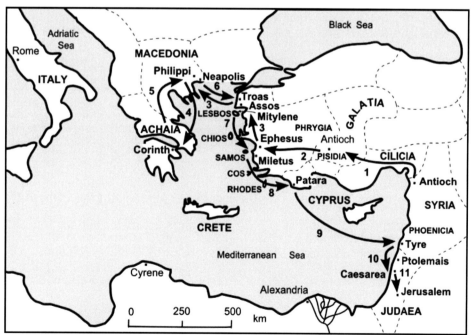

Figure 123. Map of Paul's Third Missionary Journey. Map Illustrated by Lance K. Trask)

PAUL IN EPHESUS

As mentioned above, Paul left Aquila and Priscilla in Ephesus while he returned home to Antioch. We do not know why Paul refused to stay longer in Ephesus on his Second Missionary Journey. Perhaps he was tired; perhaps he wanted to travel to Jerusalem and report back on all that had transpired during his mission in Greece. At any rate, late in 54 A.D., a rested Paul set out on what would become his Third Missionary Journey (Figure 123). The Apostle traveled from Syria through Cilicia and Galatia, likely stopping and visiting with the believers in all the churches in the region. He then headed west to Ephesus where he would spend most of the next three years, the longest period of time Paul would spend at any one place after starting his missionary travels.

Upon arriving at Ephesus, Paul met with some new believers but found that their belief was not exactly according to the Gospel:

"Paul took the road through the interior and arrived at Ephesus. There he found some disciples and asked them, 'Did you receive the Holy Spirit when you believed?' They answered, 'No, we have not even heard that there is a Holy Spirit'. So Paul asked, 'Then what baptism did you receive?' 'John's baptism', they replied. Paul said, 'John's baptism was a baptism of repentance. He told people to believe in the one coming after him, that is, Jesus.' On hearing this, they were baptized in the name of the Lord Jesus. When Paul placed his hands on them, the Holy Spirit came on them, and they spoke in tongues and prophesied. There were about twelve men in all." (Acts 19:1-7)

Paul continued his mission, first going into the local synagogue and preaching to the Jews and the God-fearing Greeks as was his custom. Some scholars estimate that the Jewish population of Ephesus during the first century A.D. may have been as large as 10,000, so Paul would clearly have had good-sized audiences. But after about three months, some of the Jews refused to listen to Paul any further and began to publicly malign Jesus and His Gospel. At this point Paul left the synagogue and began to preach solely to the Gentiles, as he had done in Corinth. Acts 19 tells us that his regular place of meeting was in the "lecture hall of Tyrannus". We do not know precisely who Tyrannus was other than a recognized teacher. The name appears to be a derivative of the word tyrant, perhaps even a nickname given to him by his students. Some versions of the Book of Acts say that Paul would preach daily from "eleven in the morning until four in the afternoon", perhaps during Tyrannus' break for lunch and a bath.

To date, the location of the Hall of Tyrannus has not been found. However, when visiting the site in the spring of 2017, the author was told that Turkish archeologists believe it is along the Arcadian Way, somewhere between the theater and the harbor front. Future archeological investigations are planned for this area, depending upon the availability of government funding.

In addition to preaching the Gospel, Paul worked a large number of miracles of healing while in Ephesus. Luke tells us that even handkerchiefs and aprons that had touched Paul were taken to the sick and their illness were cured (Acts 19:11-12). He also drove out evil spirits and confronted people who were practicing sorcery, some even in the name of Jesus. Confronted by Paul and the power of the Holy Spirit, many of these people repented, bringing their magic scrolls and burning them publicly.

Paul also used Ephesus as a base to extend the reach of the church inland into Asia Minor. This missionary outreach of the church in Ephesus is confirmed by the greetings sent by "the churches of Asia" to Corinth (I Corinthians 16:19). Paul mentions the names of three of these churches: Colossae, Laodicea, and Hierapolis (Colossians 4:13). Paul did not personally evangelize in these three cities in the Lycus River Valley (Colossians 2:1). The churches were founded by Epaphras, a native of Colossae (Colossians 4:12-13) who had been commissioned by Paul (Colossians 1:7). This seemed to reflect Paul's evolving ministerial strategy. He knew first-hand how difficult it was to start a church from scratch as a stranger in a new city. He also had seen how effective people like Lydia could be in spreading the Gospel and growing a church. So Paul used natives of the area, like Epaphras, whom he trained personally and then sent out to spread the Good News. And, if needed, Paul would write letters to those churches, giving them further instruction and encouragement.

We do not know if Paul also evangelized the other churches in the region in the same manner as those in the Lycus Valley. Ephesus and Laodicea are two of the Seven Churches of Revelation, and the remaining five (Smyrna, Pergamum, Thyatira, Sardis and Philadelphia) are all connected to Ephesus via a mail route road system. Thus it is certainly feasible that Paul may have commissioned followers to go to these cities and preach the Gospel in his stead.

Paul also used his time in Ephesus to write letters to all the churches he had helped found, giving them advice on how to apply the Gospel to daily life, and how to overcome internal problems including how to select elders and how to treat fellow church members who had somehow gone astray. During the nearly three years in Ephesus, Paul is believed to have written his "angry letter" to the Galatians counseling them not to believe the Judaizers; several letters to the Philippians, which have come down to us as a single epistle; the letter to the Colossians; Philemon; his "previous letter to Corinth", referred to in I Corinthians 5:9 but not preserved in Scripture; I Corinthians; and II Corinthians. Paul may have written more letters but the above are the ones that many scholars (but not all) agree were written during his stay in Ephesus.

At the end of the three years, Paul decided to make another trip through Greece and also visit Rome. He sent Timothy and Erastus to Macedonia while he stayed at Ephesus a little longer (Acts 19:21-22). But before Paul left Ephesus, he was involved in what turned out to be a riot:

"About that time there arose a great disturbance about the Way. A silversmith named Demetrius, who made silver shrines of Artemis, brought in a lot of business for the craftsmen there. He called them together, along with the workers in related trades, and said: 'You know, my friends, that we receive a good income from this business. And you see and hear how this fellow Paul has convinced and led astray large numbers of people here in Ephesus and in practically the whole province of Asia. He says that gods made by human hands are no gods at all. There is danger not only that our trade will lose its good name, but also that the temple of the great goddess Artemis will be discredited; and the goddess herself, who is worshiped throughout the province of Asia and the world, will be robbed of her divine majesty.' When they heard this, they were furious and began shouting: 'Great is Artemis of the Ephesians!' Soon the whole city was in an uproar. The people seized Gaius and Aristarchus, Paul's traveling companions from Macedonia, and all of them rushed into the theater

together. Paul wanted to appear before the crowd, but the disciples would not let him. Even some of the officials of the province, friends of Paul, sent him a message begging him not to venture into the theater. The assembly was in confusion: Some were shouting one thing, some another. Most of the people did not even know why they were there. The Jews in the crowd pushed Alexander to the front, and they shouted instructions to him. He motioned for silence in order to make a defense before the people. But when they realized he was a Jew, they all shouted in unison for about two hours: 'Great is Artemis of the Ephesians!' The city clerk quieted the crowd and said: 'Fellow Ephesians, doesn't all the world know that the city of Ephesus is the guardian of the temple of the great Artemis and of her image, which fell from heaven? Therefore, since these facts are undeniable, you ought to calm down and not do anything rash. You have brought these men here, though they have neither robbed temples nor blasphemed our goddess. If, then, Demetrius and his fellow craftsmen have a grievance against anybody, the courts are open and there are proconsuls. They can press charges. If there is anything further you want to bring up, it must be settled in a legal assembly. As it is, we are in danger of being charged with rioting because of what happened today. In that case we would not be able to account for this commotion, since there is no reason for it.' After he had said this, he dismissed the assembly." (Acts 19:23-41)

Paul escaped being hurt by the mob by the quick thinking of the city clerk. Starting a riot in a Roman city was a serious offense, and both the city officials and the silversmiths knew that the authorities in Rome would harshly punish all involved. But the episode demonstrates how revered the Asian goddess Artemis was in Ephesus and the uphill battle Paul was facing not just in preaching monotheism, but also in preaching the Gospel of Christ.

After the near riot in the amphitheater, Paul gave his followers encouragement and then bid them farewell. He then traveled throughout Macedonia and down to Corinth, spending another three months in that city. After being warned of a plot against their lives, Paul and his companions retraced their path back up through Macedonia and then over to Troas. They boarded another ship at Assos and sailed to Samos and then down past Ephesus to Miletus (see

Figure 123). Paul bypassed Ephesus on purpose as he was carrying a large sum of money for the people of Judea and he wanted to arrive in Jerusalem before Pentecost. However, not forgetting his followers in Ephesus, he sent word to the church elders to travel to Miletus (about 50 miles south of Ephesus) and meet with him:

"From Miletus, Paul sent to Ephesus for the elders of the church. When they arrived, he said to them: 'You know how I lived the whole time I was with you, from the first day I came into the province of Asia. I served the Lord with great humility and with tears and in the midst of severe testing by the plots of my Jewish opponents. You know that I have not hesitated to preach anything that would be helpful to you but have taught you publicly and from house to house. I have declared to both Jews and Greeks that they must turn to God in repentance and have faith in our Lord Jesus. And now, compelled by the Spirit, I am going to Jerusalem, not knowing what will happen to me there. I only know that in every city the Holy Spirit warns me that prison and hardships are facing me. However, I consider my life worth nothing to me; my only aim is to finish the race and complete the task the Lord Jesus has given me – the task of testifying to the good news of God's grace. Now I know that none of you among whom I have gone about preaching the kingdom will ever see me again. Therefore, I declare to you today that I am innocent of the blood of any of you. For I have not hesitated to proclaim to you the whole will of God. Keep watch over yourselves and all the flock of which the Holy Spirit has made you overseers. Be shepherds of the church of God, which he bought with his own blood. I know that after I leave, savage wolves will come in among you and will not spare the flock. Even from your own number men will arise and distort the truth in order to draw away disciples after them. So be on your guard! Remember that for three years I never stopped warning each of you night and day with tears. Now I commit you to God and to the word of his grace, which can build you up and give you an inheritance among all those who are sanctified. I have not coveted anyone's silver or gold or clothing. You yourselves know that these hands of mine have supplied my own needs and the needs of my companions. In everything I did, I showed you that by this kind of hard work we must help the weak,

remembering the words the Lord Jesus himself said: 'It is more blessed to give than to receive.' When Paul had finished speaking, he knelt down with all of them and prayed. They all wept as they embraced him and kissed him. What grieved them most was his statement that they would never see his face again. Then they accompanied him to the ship." (Acts 20:17-37)

With that final farewell, Paul sailed on toward Jerusalem and never again returned to Ephesus. However, he did not forget his believers there and while in Rome under house arrest, he penned his letter to the Ephesians.

In addition to the Apostle Paul and his ministry, Ephesus is important to two other notable Biblical figures, the Apostle John and Mary, the mother of Jesus. The early church historian, Eusebios, wrote that John was expelled from Jerusalem around 37 A.D. He evangelized throughout Asia Minor for five years and then settled in Ephesus where he wrote his gospel. Tradition says that John took Mary along with him to Ephesus. Mary died shortly thereafter and was "buried" in Ephesus. I say "buried" because according to the tradition of the Roman Catholic and Greek / Russian Orthodox Church, Mary was bodily taken up into heaven either just before or just after her death, leaving no body to bury. A site in Ephesus reputed to be Mary's house is preserved and venerated by believers today.

In the latter part of the first century A.D., the Apostle John became the leader of the church in Ephesus. From there, he was exiled to the island of Patmos, where he received and wrote The Revelation. He returned after the death of the Emperor Domitian (96 A.D.) to spend his final days in the city. There is a church today over the place where the apostle is reportedly buried.

8 RHODES, CRETE AND MALTA

In completing his Third Missionary Journey as well as on his final trip to Rome, Paul landed at a number of islands in the eastern and central Mediterranean. On three of these islands, Rhodes, Crete and Malta, there is a strong Pauline tradition that he not only stopped there but evangelized and started churches which exist to this day.

RHODES

"After we had torn ourselves away from them, we put out to sea and sailed straight to Kos. The next day we went to Rhodes and from there to Patara. We found a ship crossing over to Phoenicia, went on board and set sail. After sighting Cyprus and passing to the south of it, we sailed on to Syria. We landed at Tyre, where our ship was to unload its cargo. We sought out the disciples there and stayed with them seven days." (Acts 20:1-4)

The above one-line mention of Paul's ship landing on the island of Rhodes before sailing on to Phoenicia (modern Lebanon) constitutes Luke's only mention of Paul being on the island. He does not go into any detail of their activities there nor how long they stayed. In the first century A.D., merchant ships usually sailed point-to-point, traveling short distances; carrying, unloading and loading cargo at each stop. Depending upon the amount of cargo held in the ship, the process of unloading and reloading could take anywhere from several days to a week or more.

There are two local traditions as to where Paul landed on Rhodes. After passing Kos (famous for its Sanctuary to Asclepius), Paul's ship passed the peninsula of Cnidus and came to Rhodes. One tradition has it that Paul's ship arrived at the city of Rhodes, famous for its Colossus, one of the Seven Wonders of the Ancient World. The Colossus was a bronze statue of the god Apollo built between 304-284 B.C. Its height was between 90 and 120 feet and the statue is estimated to have weighed close to 250 tons. There is some belief that it may have served as a lighthouse for the harbor. According to Strabo, a massive earthquake in 225 B.C.

broke the statue at its knees, and because of an oracle of future doom, the people of Rhodes never rebuilt it. There is no archeological evidence as to its exact location as its remains were sold in 656 A.D. to a Jewish merchant from Syria who used 900 camels to cart the remaining pieces away.

The Rhodians maintain that the Apostle stayed for some time in their city and preached, bringing many people into the new faith. Before he left, Paul appointed a man named Prochorus to be the Bishop of the island.

Another tradition has it that Paul's contact with the island was at Lindos, one of the three ancient cities of the island. Lindos is located about 34 miles from the town of Rhodes. Lindos was founded near the beginning of the third millenni-

Figure 124. The Acropolis at Lindos, Island of Rhodes.

Table 16. Key Dates and Events for Lindos Through the First Century

Date	Event
ca. 5000 B.C.	Island of Rhodes inhabited by farmers migrating from the Middle East
ca. 3000-1150 B.C.	City of Lindos is founded
ca. 800-700 B.C.	Dorian Greek invasion; Lindos becomes part of the "Dorian Hexapolis"
ca. 700-500 B.C.	Lindos becomes a natural meeting place and center of commerce between the Greeks and the Phoenicians
ca. 408 B.C.	Lindos' importance begins to decline after the founding of the city of Rhodes
ca. 342-300 B.C.	The Temple of Athena build on the Acropolis at Lindos; the Acropolis and its temple becomes the second most significant after Athens
43 B.C.	Rhodes (and Lindos) becomes part of the Roman Empire
ca. 57 A.D.	Paul makes a brief stop on the island of Rhodes (probably Lindos) in route to Jerusalem; St. Paul's Bay adjacent to the Acropolis of Lindos memorializes this stopover

um B.C., primarily because there was a naturally defensible acropolis adjacent to an excellent natural harbor (Table 16; Figure 124). Because of the island of Rhodes' location, Lindos became a nexus of sea trade between the island, other islands in the eastern Mediterranean, and with the Phoenicians. In the eight century B.C., Lindos was occupied by Dorian Greeks and the city-state became a Greek colony. As a natural meeting place between the Greek and Phoenicians worlds, Lindos thrived for the next several centuries. However, when the city of Rhodes was built with a larger harbor on the Greek side of the island, Lindos' importance began to wane.

Figure 125. Temple of Athena, Lindos Acropolis, Rhodes.

A large temple to the goddess Athena was built toward the end of the fourth century B.C. on the acropolis at Lindos which became the second most important site for the worship of Athena, surpassed only by Athens (Figure 125). The island of Rhodes became a Roman possession in 43 B.C. and Lindos' importance continued to wane relative to the newer and larger port at Rhodes. The tradition that Paul's ship landed at Lindos centers on the small, naturally protected harbor adjacent to the

Figure 126. View of St. Paul's Bay from the Acropolis at Lindos.

acropolis which is known to this day as St. Paul's Bay (Figure 126). There is a small Greek Orthodox chapel on the edge of the bay which commemorates Paul's landing and preaching across the island.

CRETE

The other two island stops for Paul occurred during his final voyage to Rome (Figure 127). After spending two years awaiting trial in Caesarea (ca. 57-59 A.D.) (see Chapter 1), Paul was sent to Rome via ship accompanied by a Roman Centurion as his guard:

"When it was decided that we would sail for Italy, Paul and some other prisoners were handed over to a centurion named Julius, who belonged to the Imperial Regiment. We boarded a ship from Adramyttium about to sail for ports along the coast of the province of Asia, and we put out to sea. Aristarchus, a Macedonian from Thessalonica, was with us. The next day we landed at Sidon; and Julius, in kindness to Paul, allowed him to go to his friends so they might provide for his needs. From there we put out to sea again and passed to the lee of Cyprus because the winds were against us. When we had sailed across the open sea off the coast of Cilicia and Pamphylia, we landed at Myra in Lycia. There the centurion found an Alexandrian ship sailing for Italy and put us on board. We made slow headway for many days and had difficulty arriving off Cnidus. When the wind did not allow us to hold our course, we sailed to the lee of Crete, opposite Salmone. We moved along the coast with difficulty and came to a place called Fair Havens, near the town of Lasea." (Acts 27:1-8)

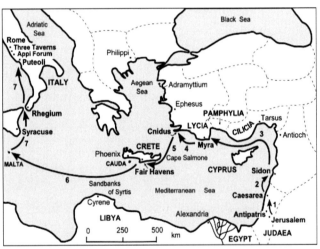

Figure 127. Map of Paul's Final Journey to Rome. (Map Illustrated by Lance K. Trask)

Note that Paul was entrusted to a Centurion (a leader of a "Century" – a military unit roughly equivalent to a modern Company; Roman Centuries typically had about 80 men but the number fluctuated greatly over time) named Julius who was a member of the Imperial Regiment. We do not know exactly what Luke meant by this but most probably Julius was a member of the Praetorian Guard who had been in Judea for some assignment and was traveling back to his home in Rome. The Praetorian Guard was created to protect the city of Rome, and in particular, to be the body guard of Caesar and the Senate. To be a Centurion within the Praetorian Guard was a rank of some note.

Paul's ship followed the standard coast-hugging, point-to-point course of most ships of the day, first sailing along the southern coast of Asia Minor, and then from the Cnidus Peninsula southwestward to the island of Crete. Some scholars maintain that Paul sailed from Caesarea

near the end of August in 59 A.D. The Greek Orthodox text of Acts states that the voyage from Caesarea to Myra took 15 days. Note that their original ship sailed only as far as Myra and the Centurion Julius then had to find an Egyptian ship that was heading west toward Italy. Considering the very slow progress the ship made after that, and the fact that Acts 27:9 states that it was already after the Day of Atonement, Paul's landing in Crete was likely around the first week of October.

Figure 128. The Port of Fair Havens on the Island of Crete. (Photo Courtesy of On Wings of Eagles Christian Tours, Brighton, Colorado)

During the first century A.D., ships typically did not sail across the Mediterranean after mid-September. The safe sailing season for crossing the Mediterranean was considered to be between May 27 and September 14. Most ships did not cross the open Mediterranean after the fall because the seasonal winds came from the north and drove ships against the coast of Africa. Shipping typically closed from November 11 to March 10. Travel in the spring between March and May and in the fall between September and November was possible, but was considered risky. It was with great difficulty and many days of sailing that they finally landed at the port of Fair Havens in Crete (Figure 128).

The fact that the Centurion found passage for them on a ship from Alexandria indicates that this was a grain ship (Rome depended heavily on Egypt's grain shipments) trying to squeeze in one final run before winter. There is some indication that the Emperor Nero was trying to stave off a grain shortage in Rome and the ship carrying Paul and his companions may have been part of that effort.

Fair Havens, known in Greek as Kaloi Limenes or Kalous Limionas, is a bay with a very small village on the southern coast of Crete. The bay is small and not suitable for wintering a ship because the bay is exposed to the wind and sea. The owner of the ship and Julius decided to try and sail further west to a harbor named Phoenix but Paul, who by this time was a seasoned sea traveler, cautioned against sailing further west. Disregarding Paul's advice, the ship sailed on which eventually led to their being shipwrecked on the island of Malta.

The people of Crete have a number of traditions about the Apostle Paul's missionary activities while on the island. One tradition has it that Paul was freed from imprisonment in Rome and returned to Crete to evangelize. During this time, he was said to have banished all the poisonous snakes from the island. The story is so similar to the one about Paul and the viper in Malta that it seems that somehow the same story morphed into a Cretan legend as well. However, in writing to Titus, Paul says, "this is why I left you in Crete, that you might amend what is defective, and appoint elders in every town as I directed you" (Titus 1:5). This suggests that the author of the epistle spent some time on Crete, and if Paul is indeed the author of the book of Titus, then he must have spent time there during the voyage to Rome or at a later date.

In the letter to Titus, the author goes on to say, "Cretans are always liars, evil beats, lazy gluttons'. This testimony is true. Therefore rebuke them sharply." (Titus 1:12-13). If these words are from Paul, this would seem rather untactful, especially if trying to convert people to a new faith. The original quote is one from Epimenides of Knossos (sixth century B.C.) and has come down in history almost as an epithet regarding the Cretans.

Outside of the brief mention of Fair Havens in Acts and the reference to Cretans in the letter to Titus, there is no other scriptural record of Paul spending any time on the island. Most is local tradition, and there are a number of churches on the island that commemorate the Apostle's missionary work there.

MALTA

Despite Paul's warning about the weather, the Alexandrian ship pressed on westwards:

"But the centurion, instead of listening to what Paul said, followed the advice of the pilot and of the owner of the ship. Since the harbor was unsuitable to winter in, the majority decided that we should sail on, hoping to reach Phoenix and winter there. This was a harbor in Crete, facing both southwest and northwest." (Acts 27:11-12)

As Paul had feared, when they began to sail westwards the ship was caught in a storm which drove them to the south toward the coast of Africa. Off the coast of Libya there are two major sandbanks, the Greater and Lesser Syrtes, which were notorious for causing ship wrecks because of their hidden nature until almost on top of them, and very strong circular tides (3 knots or more) which tend to sweep ships into the banks. These are precisely the conditions that Paul and his shipmates encountered:

> *"When a gentle south wind began to blow, they saw their opportunity; so they weighed anchor and sailed along the shore of Crete. Before very long, a wind of hurricane force, called the Northeaster, swept down from the island. The ship was caught by the storm and could not head into the wind; so we gave way to it and were driven along. As we passed to the lee of a small island called Cauda, we were hardly able to make the lifeboat secure, so the men hoisted it aboard. Then they passed ropes under the ship itself to hold it together. Because they were afraid they would run aground on the sandbars of Syrtis, they lowered the sea anchor and let the ship be driven along. We took such a violent battering from the storm that the next day they began to throw the cargo overboard. On the third day, they threw the ship's tackle overboard with their own hands. When neither sun nor stars appeared for many days and the storm continued raging, we finally gave up all hope of being saved. After they had gone a long time without food, Paul stood up before them and said: 'Men, you should have taken my advice not to sail from Crete; then you would have spared yourselves this damage and loss. But now I urge you to keep up your courage, because not one of you will be lost; only the ship will be destroyed. Last night an angel of the God to whom I belong and whom I serve stood beside me and said, 'Do not be afraid, Paul. You must stand trial before Caesar; and God has graciously given you the lives of all who sail with you.' So keep up your courage, men, for I have faith in God that it will happen just as he told me. Nevertheless, we must run aground on some island."* (Acts 27:13-26)

The storm continued to push Paul's ship south and the crew, using sea anchors to stabilize the ship, attempted to use the wind to move them westward as they were unable to sail north to reach the western edge of Crete. Ships sailing from Crete typically sailed north and west to reach Italy. However, the storm was taking them literally into uncharted waters.

"On the fourteenth night we were still being driven across the Adriatic Sea, when about midnight the sailors sensed they were approaching land. They took soundings and found that the water was a hundred and twenty feet deep. A short time later they took soundings again and found it was ninety feet deep. Fearing that we would be dashed against the rocks, they dropped four anchors from the stern and prayed for daylight. In an attempt to escape from the ship, the sailors let the lifeboat down into the sea, pretending they were going to lower some anchors from the bow. Then Paul said to the centurion and the soldiers, 'Unless these men stay with the ship, you cannot be saved.' So the soldiers cut the ropes that held the lifeboat and let it drift away. Just before dawn Paul urged them all to eat. 'For the last fourteen days,' he said, 'you have been in constant suspense and have gone without food – you haven't eaten anything. Now I urge you to take some food. You need it to survive. Not one of you will lose a single hair from his head.' After he said this, he took some bread and gave thanks to God in front of them all. Then he broke it and began to eat. They were all encouraged and ate some food themselves. Altogether there were 276 of us on board. When they had eaten as much as they wanted, they lightened the ship by throwing the grain into the sea. When daylight came, they did not recognize the land, but they saw a bay with a sandy beach, where they decided to run the ship aground if they could. Cutting loose the anchors, they left them in the sea and at the same time untied the ropes that held the rudders. Then they hoisted the foresail to the wind and made for the beach. But the ship struck a sandbar and ran aground. The bow stuck fast and would not move, and the stern was broken to pieces by the pounding of the surf. The soldiers planned to kill the prisoners to prevent any of them from swimming away and escaping.

But the centurion wanted to spare Paul's life and kept them from carrying out their plan. He ordered those who could swim to jump overboard first and get to land. The rest were to get there on planks or on other pieces of the ship. In this way everyone reached land safely." (Acts 27:27-44)

Confirmation of Luke's account of the storm and the difficulty in trying to sail through it comes from modern navigational records. A ship in the Mediterranean will normally drift about 1.5 miles per hour, which tallies almost perfectly with the distance from the island of Cauda (south of Crete) to Malta over a period of 14 days.

There were two basic types of ships that existed in the Roman Empire during the first century A.D. – military and merchant – and both types avoided sailing across the open Mediterranean during the winter season.

The Roman navy and its merchant marine fleet were instrumental in Rome's conquest of the Mediterranean and the maintenance of the Empire, but they never enjoyed the same level of prestige as the army. In fact, the navy never existed as a separate force; it was always viewed as an adjunct arm of the army. The birth of Roman naval power goes back to 311 B.C. when the government ordered the construction of 20 ships, mostly copies of Greek Triremes (ships with three decks of oars manned by one man per oar). The fact that these ships were a direct copy of another nation's ships is characteristic of Roman sea power. Throughout the long history of the Empire, Rome relied almost exclusively on other nation's ships (Greece and Egypt), their design, and their naval manpower.

Expansion across the Mediterranean in the second and third centuries B.C. inevitably led to a conflict between Rome and the major seafaring nation of the time, Carthage, an independent state developed from a Phoenician colony in North Africa. In 261 B.C., the Roman Senate ordered the construction of 20 Triremes based on the Greek design and 100 Quin-queremes (five decks of oars with at least one man, and frequently more, per oar – the battleships of their day). Prior to construction of the ships, a Carthaginian Quinquereme accidently beached itself on Roman territory. The Romans captured the ship intact, took it apart, and back-engineered its technology.

Naval battles at the time were based on speed, maneuverability, and ramming. All ships were fitted with a large bronze ram attached to the bow which was the principal weapon of the ship. The Romans quickly realized that they could not match the speed and skill of the Carthaginian fleet, so they devised a new weapon system called a "corvus" or "crow". The corvus was a long boarding plank with a large iron spike at one end. Roman ships would sail next to their adversaries, swing the corvus over the side and attach it to the deck of the opposing ship. Roman Legionnaires, on board in the function of Marines, would race across onto the other ship's deck and turn a naval battle into a land battle. The lightly armed sailors of the opposing ship were no match for the more heavily armed and well-trained Legionnaires. The Romans later invented a weapon called the harpax, a catapult thrown grappling hook system which replaced the more bulky corvus.

After conquering Carthage, the Roman navy was reduced in size to about 100 major warships whose job was to protect the merchant fleet from pirates and escort Roman soldiers from one place to another. While all Roman vessels were equipped with a large sail, the bulk of the crew were rowers (*remiges*). Contrary to popular depictions in the movies, most rowers were not slaves but freed men. If they were not free when they were assigned to the service, they were typically freed prior to joining a ship. The rowers were classified as soldiers (*milites*), and received full Roman citizenship, regular army pay, and a substantial pension at the end of their 26-28 service term. A typical Trireme had a crew of about 200, of which 170 would be rowers. Each ship had a Centurion, who commanded the Marine fighting force, and a Trier-archus, who served as the ship's Captain and frequently navigator as well. Squadrons of ten or more warships were commanded by a Nauarchus (Commodore) and fleets would be command-ed by a Consul from the patrician class.

Roman warships tended to be flat-bottomed for speed and maneuverability whereas merchant ships were more V-shaped with deeper drafts. The shape of the hull was purposefully designed in order to be able to stack the maximum amount of the elongate, oval-shaped amphorae – the standard carrying vessel for many products. Merchant ships typically had two sails, one from a large center mast and a smaller forward sail to aid in maneuverability. Rome maintained a large merchant fleet but almost all of it was in private hands and not controlled by the government per se. In 218 B.C., the Senate passed a law which stated that all high ranking Roman officials could not own any vessel which carried more than three hundred amphorae. This law was in accordance with the tradition that patricians didn't dirty themselves with commerce but focused on amassing wealth through land control and farming.

Merchant vessels were typically point-to-point carriers, transporting cargoes relatively short distances, off-loading that cargo, reloading, and then carrying on to the next destination. As a result, most ship voyages tended to hug the coast lines and did not cross the open sea. When laden with a large cargo, many of the ships did not maneuver well in rough seas and could capsize easily in a storm.

Ships were designed to carry cargo and not passengers. However, passengers would be taken aboard, especially good paying passengers who needed to travel quickly to relatively short destinations. There might be a single small deck cabin at the stern of the ship but most of the ship's crew, and any passengers, either slept on deck if it was warm, or in the hold in what space was available in and around the ship's cargo. Sanitation was minimal at best, with most crewmen relieving themselves over the side of the ship. This was usually done near the bow (the head) so that wave action would hopefully wash away whatever sewage was stuck to the ship.

Given that the Mediterranean is known for sudden, violent storms, ship travel was dangerous, dirty and offered few comforts except the speed of travel. The fact that Luke devotes an entire chapter to the storm and the eventual shipwreck demonstrates what a terrifying ordeal it was, especially for Luke who may never have experienced being shipwrecked before.

Sailing the Mediterranean during a storm could be very dangerous, not only because of the rough seas but also because the cloudy weather made it impossible to fix one's location with any degree of accuracy. So far, over 1,000 wrecks of Greek, Minoan, Phoenician and Roman ships have been found off the coasts of Europe, Asia Minor, Palestine and North Africa. And boats were not just in danger while at sea. The Roman historian Tacitus records that 200 ships carrying corn were destroyed in a single storm while harbored in Ostia, Rome's port on the Mediterranean.

Paul's ship hit the rocks off the coast of an unknown island and no fewer than 276 people either swam ashore or floated in on the waves using pieces of the ship as rafts. They now needed to find out where they were and where they could winter until the spring when hopefully they could find a new ship in order to continue on their journey to Italy:

"Once safely on shore, we found out that the island was called Malta. The islanders showed us unusual kindness. They built a fire and welcomed us all

because it was raining and cold. Paul gathered a pile of brushwood and, as he put it on the fire, a viper, driven out by the heat, fastened itself on his hand. When the islanders saw the snake hanging from his hand, they said to each other, 'This man must be a murderer; for though he escaped from the sea, the goddess Justice has not allowed him to live.' But Paul shook the snake off into the fire and suffered no ill effects. The people expected him to swell up or suddenly fall dead; but after waiting a long time and seeing nothing unusual happen to him, they changed their minds and said he was a god." (Acts 28:1-6)

They discovered they were on an island called Malta, quite possibly a place that neither Paul nor Luke had ever heard of. The people did not speak Greek or Latin, which in the Roman world of the first century A.D. meant that they were "Barbarians". Malta consists of three islands, the large island of Malta, the island of Gozo to its north, and in between, the tiny almost uninhabited island of Comino. The islands were first inhabited around 5500 B.C. when Neolithic farmers migrated from the Middle East across the Mediterranean. Malta's original inhabitants are believed to have crossed the 58 miles from Sicily in small boats, bringing with

Table 17. Key Dates and Events for Malta Through the First Century A.D.

Date	Event
ca. 5500 B.C.	Island of Malta first inhabited by farmers migrating from Sicily via the Middle East through Europe
ca. 3600-2500 B.C.	Megalithic Temples built over the islands of Malta and Gozo
ca. 800-450 B.C.	Island strongly influenced by traders from Greece, Phoenicia and the Etruscans
ca. 450-250 B.C.	Malta becomes a trading outpost and colony for Carthage
218 B.C.	Malta is captured by the Romans during the Second Punic War (218-201 B.C.); the island is named "Melita" which is Latin for honey
ca. 59 A.D.	Apostle Paul is shipwrecked on the island in route to Rome; the traditional site, St. Paul's Bay, is located on the northeast side of the main island; Paul stays on the island for three months; is bitten by a viper but does not die which wins him many converts
ca. 60 A.D.	Paul sails for Rome via Sicily

them cereal grains and livestock (sheep, goats, cattle). By 3600 B.C., these people had constructed huge megalithic temples all across the island, many of them larger in size and scope than Stonehenge and a 1000 years older than the famous British monument. The megalithic culture thrived for a millennium and then suddenly disappeared around 2500 B.C.

Malta was then inhabited by a series of peoples: the Phoenicians, the Carthaginians, the Romans, the Byzantines, and later by Arabs, Ottoman Turks, Normans, Spaniards, Italians, French and most recently, the English (Table 17). The people speak English today, but the local language is Malti, which is a strange and almost unintelligible combination of Arabic, Latin, Italian and other European languages. Malta was controlled by the Carthaginians when the Romans captured it during second Punic War (218-201 B.C.). The Romans named the islands "Melita", which is the Latin word for honey. Malta produces a honey with a very unique flavor and its name is believed to have derived from this word for honey.

Figure 129. St. Paul's Bay, Island of Malta. (Photo Courtesy of Ian Trickle)

The precise area in which the Apostle Paul and the crew of the Alexandrian ship landed is not known for sure, but local tradition states that the landing point was on the northeastern side of the large island of Malta at a place now known as St. Paul's Bay (Figure 129). Luke's account is not very specific, indicating only that the sailors saw a bay with a sandy beach but were not able to run the ship onto the beach because they first hit a sandbar. The northeast coast of Malta is characterized by alternating bays and headlands. Between the Melieha Ridge and Wadija Ridge, the Pwales Valley opens onto St. Paul's Bay. There are very few sandy beaches along Malta's eastern coast but St. Paul's Bay does fit Luke's description. The bay has two small, rocky islands at its mouth which are believed to be the place where the ship ran aground and then was broken up by the waves. Malta (all three islands) is only about 20 miles in length and it was a miracle that the ship managed to make landfall on the island when there was a high probability they would have missed it completely and been swept against the rocky shores of nearby Tunisia. Paul and Luke would have seen their safe arrival on Malta and then the hospitality given to them by the local inhabitants as a clear sign of God's gracious provision and providence.

The local Maltese people were amazed when Paul was bitten by a viper and then did not die. There are three types of snakes native to Malta and none are venomous, but the local inhabitants believe the snake that bit the Apostle was a Leopard Snake which does in fact look like a viper. His reputation grew further when he healed the father of the senior Roman official on the island:

"There was an estate nearby that belonged to Publius, the chief official of the island. He welcomed us to his home and showed us generous hospitality for three days. His father was sick in bed, suffering from fever and dysentery. Paul went in to see him and, after prayer, placed his hands on him and healed him. When this had happened, the rest of the sick on the island came and were cured. They honored us in many ways; and when we were ready to sail, they furnished us with the supplies we needed." (Acts 28:7-10)

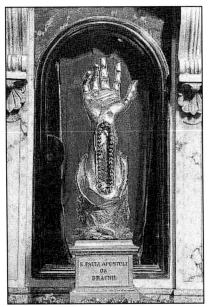

Figure 130. Entrance to Church of St. Paul's Shipwreck, Valletta, Malta.

Figure 131. Reliquary Containing the Hand of St. Paul, Valletta, Malta. (Photo Courtesy of Ian Trickle)

Luke says that they stayed three months on the island, which would have been the very minimum amount of time for wintering before sailing. As Malta is a series of three isolated islands, and it was winter with no ship traffic, the Centurion Julius may have afforded Paul and Luke a fair amount of freedom. Perhaps the whole island of Malta became an unofficial prison and Paul was able to have an extended ministry. Certainly the tradition on Malta would support this. For a relatively short stay by Paul, Malta has one of the strongest Pauline traditions outside of Rome. No less than 50 churches on the island claim to have a link to the Apostle. The largest and most important of these is the Church of St. Paul's Shipwreck in Valletta, the capital of Malta (Figure 130). While very modest on the outside, the inside of the church has a large number of murals depicting Paul's shipwreck and his ministry on Malta. More importantly, in the southern transept is a reliquary which reportedly contains part of the right hand and wrist bone of the Apostle, a gift from the Vatican in 1823 (Figure 131). There is also a portion of the pillar to which Paul was chained when he was executed. Pope Paul VI simply referred to Malta as "the island of St. Paul".

Near St. Paul's Bay is the town of Rabat, former capital of Malta. At Rabat, a significant Roman villa and baths have been excavated. The area is reputed to have been the home of Publius, the Roman official whose father Paul healed. Maltese tradition is that Publius not only converted to Christianity, but later became the first Bishop of the island and is considered by the Maltese to be a saint. In Rabat, beneath the parish church of St. Paul, are several caves. According to local tradition, these caves are where Paul lived, healed those that traveled to see him, and preached during his stay on the island.

After three months, the Centurion Julius found the travelers another Alexandrian grain ship which had wintered on Malta and booked passage for Italy:

> *"After three months we put out to sea in a ship that had wintered in the island – it was an Alexandrian ship with the figurehead of the twin gods Castor and Pollux." (Acts 28:11)*

Paul then headed for Rome, the final leg of his life's journey.

9 ROME

"We put in at Syracuse and stayed there three days. From there we set sail and arrived at Rhegium. The next day the south wind came up, and on the following day we reached Puteoli. There we found some brothers and sisters who invited us to spend a week with them. And so we came to Rome. The brothers and sisters there had heard that we were coming, and they traveled as far as the Forum of Appius and the Three Taverns to meet us. At the sight of these people Paul thanked God and was encouraged. When we got to Rome, Paul was allowed to live by himself, with a soldier to guard him." (Acts 28:12-16)

The trip from Malta to Syracuse on the east coast of the island of Sicily is about 130 miles in length. Cargo ships during the first century A.D. traveled largely at the mercy of currents and the wind; they did not have the large number of rowers that warships had as there was never a need to go to "battle speed" when moving cargo. Maritime scholars have estimated that the average speed for a Roman cargo ship was about 4.1 knots per hour, or 4.7 miles per hour. Thus the trip from Malta to Syracuse would have taken roughly a day. Luke says they then got a favorable south wind and made the 115 mile trip from Syracuse to Rhegium (modern Regio Calabria) in another day. This entailed sailing carefully through the Straits of Messina between Sicily and the toe of Italy. They then sailed northwards to Puteoli (modern Pozzuoli) located on the north side of the Bay of Naples. This is a distance of 318 miles which likely took more time than the single day recorded by Luke (Acts 28:12); but with a south wind, they certainly could have traveled faster than 4.7 miles per hour. Puteoli owed its importance to its excellent natural harbor and the fact that it was the closest large harbor to the city of Rome.

Most of the commerce from Egypt and Palestine passed through Puteoli on its way to Rome because of the limited facilities at the time in Rome's port of Ostia. Puteoli is located within the Phlegraen Fields, a large volcanic caldera which is mostly submerged offshore. It includes 24 volcanic craters which are subjected to a geologic phenomenon known as "bradyseism", in which deep magma chambers randomly fill and empty causing tremors and earthquakes that raise and lower the ground.

Once at Puteoli, the Alexandrian grain ship needed to offload its cargo to smaller ships because it was evidently too large for Rome's harbor of Ostia. This would have required at least another week so the Centurion Julius decided to complete the journey overland to Rome. Even so, he allowed Paul and Luke to meet and stay with a small group of believers in Puteoli who hosted the evangelists and took care of their needs. Also, they undoubtedly sent word to the believers in Rome that Paul was alive and well and headed for the capital.

The trip overland was made on Rome's major north-south road, the Appian Way (Figure 132). From Puteoli, the Appian Way would have led roughly 200 miles north through the cities of Capua, Minturna, Formia, Fundi, and Terracina. At the next two stops, the Forum of Appius and Three Taverns, Paul was met and escorted the rest of the way by members of the church in Rome. Paul would have come into the great city of Rome from the south side where he would have seen Rome's seven hills (Pincian, Quirinal, Viminal, Esquiline, Caelian, Aventine and Capitoline), in between which ran the Via Sacrum (the Sacred Way) into the heart of the Roman forum. Once in Rome, Luke says Paul was granted libera custodia, a version of what we would call "house arrest". He was allowed to stay in a house of his choosing with a guard instead of

Figure 132. The Appian Way Leading North into Rome. (Photo Courtesy of Louis Aulbach and Linda Gorski)

a prison cell. Roman libera custodia typically did not require the prisoner to be chained, rather that the person guarding him would provide whatever means necessary to ensure that the prisoner would not escape. As Paul was determined to have his case tried before the Emperor, the one guard and Paul's word that he would not escape were probably sufficient. Therefore, when Paul wrote that he was in chains, it probably referred to the lack of total freedom rather than being physically chained while under libera custodia.

There is archeological evidence that the area in and around Rome was inhabited from at least 3,000 B.C., but the vast amount of younger material often obscures earlier sites. The city of Rome appears to have originated as a small village of the Latini tribe somewhere in the ninth century B.C., although there is some evidence that people were living on the Palatine Hill

Table 18. Key Dates and Events for Rome Through the First Century A.D.

Date	Event
ca. 753 B.C. (April 21)	Traditional date for the founding of Rome under King Romulus; the area around Rome was inhabited as early as 3,000 B.C. and people were living on the Palatine Hill by the 10th Century B.C.; a wall was in place around a city prior to 753 B.C. so the precise origins of the city remain unknown
ca. 650 B.C.	Influence by the Etruscans
509 B.C.	Rome becomes a Republic
ca. 500-250 B.C.	Rome gains dominance over the entire Italian Peninsula
218-201 B.C.	Rome gains dominance over the western Mediterranean during the Second Punic War
ca. 200-50 B.C.	Rome conquers Greece, Asia, Syria, Palestine, Gaul Britain and part of Germany and adds them to what becomes the Roman Empire
49-27 B.C.	Julius Caesar becomes dictator in Rome and rules for five years before being assassinated in 44 B.C.; Civil War between the forces of Octavian (Caesar's nephew) and Mark Anthony versus Cassius and Brutus ends with Anthony's victory at Philippi; the victors then fight until Octavian defeats Anthony at the Battle of Actium in 31 B.C.; Octavian becomes Emperor Caesar Augustus and begins the Roman Empire in 27 B.C.
27 B.C.-14 A.D.	Reign of Augustus
14-37 A.D.	Reign of Tiberius; Jesus ministers in Galilee and Judea and is crucified; Paul is converted to Christianity on the road to Damascus
37-41 A.D.	Reign of Caligula
41-54 A.D.	Rein of Claudius; Jews are expelled from Rome (ca. 48-49 A.D.) because of unrest "at the instigation of Chrestus"
54-68 A.D.	Reign of Nero; Jews allowed to return to Rome after 54 A.D.; Paul arrives in Rome in 60 A.D. and remains for several years under house arrest waiting for his trial to be heard; put to death by beheading sometime between 62-67 A.D.
64 A.D.	Great fire of Rome; Christians blamed by Nero
68-69 A.D.	"Year of the Four Emperors" following Nero's suicide; Vespasian emerges as Emperor and rules for 10 years (69-79 A.D.); the Colosseum is built between 72-80 A.D.
79-81 A.D.	Reign of Titus; Mount Vesuvius erupts and destroys Herculaneum and Pompeii (79 A.D.)
81-96 A.D.	Rein of Domitian; great period of Christian persecution

as early as the tenth century B.C. The traditional date for the founding of Rome is April 21, 753 B.C., and the surrounding region, known as Latium, has had an uninterrupted occupation since that time (Table 18). Recent excavations have found that a wall existed around the city before 753 B.C., so its true origins are still unknown. Further complicating Roman history is the popular story of the city's founding by the twins, Romulus and Remus. The legend states that Romulus and Remus, descendants of the Trojan War survivor Aeneas, were abandoned as young children and raised by a wolf. As they grew toward manhood, they decided to build a city on the spot where they were raised, but the brothers argued and Romulus killed his brother Remus. Romulus then built the city and named it for himself. Attempts have been made to find a linguistic origin for "Rome" without any definitive answer other than the Romulus myth. Some scholars believe the name could derive from a Greek word meaning courage or bravery; it also could be connected to the root word rum meaning teat – again harkening back to the Romulus legend.

The original occupants of central Italy were various tribes of Italic language speakers from the region that included the Latini, the Sabines, the Umbrians, the Sammites, the Oscans and others. They shared the Italian peninsula with two other peoples: the Etruscans to the north and the Greeks in the south. After about 650 B.C., the Etruscans became the dominant power in Italy and expanded southward into north-central Italy. The Etruscans left a lasting impression on Rome including their temples; the triad of gods, Juno, Minerva and Jupiter; and some of their architecture. However, Rome never fully became an Etruscan city. Rome was then, and has always been, primarily a Latin city.

According to tradition, Rome became a Republic in 509 B.C., but it was many years before it became the great city of popular imagination. There were constant wars between Rome and the other Latin peoples, namely the Sabines, as well as the other peoples living on the Italian Peninsula. Rome gained regional dominance in Latium during the fifth century B.C., and eventually over all of Italy by the third century B.C. With the Punic Wars fought against the Phoenician colony of Carthage, Rome gained dominance over the western Mediterranean. Beginning in the second century B.C., the city of Rome went through a significant population expansion as a number of peoples, especially small farmers, were driven from their lands by the advent of massive, slave-operated farms called *latifundia*. The victory over the Carthaginians brought Sicily and Sardinia under Roman control – the first provinces outside of Italy to be incorporated into Rome. Spain and North Africa soon followed. The Romans then moved east, conquering all of Greece and the Greek colonies in less than 50 years. In the latter part of the first century B.C., Rome conquered Syria, Palestine and Egypt, making the Mediterranean truly a Roman lake. Gaul (modern France), part of Germany, the low countries, and Britain were also added to the growing Empire between the first century B.C. and the first century A.D. (Figure 133).

Figure 133. Map of the Roman Empire in the First Century A.D. (Map Illustrated by Lance K. Trask)

During these years of growth, Rome was governed as a Republic, with a nominal head or collective of leaders, but the real power rested with the Roman Senate. However, the growth of Roman power across the Mediterranean and Europe created new problems and new demands that the old structure of shared power and annually elected magistrates could not solve. In 49 B.C., Julius Caesar, conqueror of Gaul, marched his Legions against Rome. In the following years, he vanquished his opponents (principally Pompey the Great, conqueror of Syria and Palestine) and set himself up as dictator of Rome. Many of the members of the Roman Senate did not want to see their power diminished and placed into the hand of a single man, so Julius Caesar was assassinated by his erstwhile colleagues in 44 B.C. The Senate tried to re-establish the Roman Republic but its champions, Marcus Junius Brutus and Gaius Cassius Longinus were defeated by a combined army of Caesar's chief lieutenant, Marcus Antonius (Marc Anthony) and Caesar's nephew, Octavian.

A loose confederation of power was established with Octavian ruling in Rome and the western part of the Empire, and Anthony ruling in the east. One of the first acts undertaken by Octavian to help cement his leadership position with the people was to hold a month long series of games starting in July, 44 B.C. Octavian let it be known that the games were being held in honor of his great-uncle, Julius Caesar, and moreover, were being completely paid for at Octavian's expense. The move was a savvy one as Octavian was by no means assured of a future role in the leadership of Rome. It was what happened during the games that firmly set him on the path toward becoming the future unchallenged leader of the Roman Empire. The Roman historian Suetonius reports that during the course of the games, a comet (stella crinita) became visible for seven days in a row. The comet was apparently so bright that it could be seen during the day, starting about 11 AM. While the Senate had doubts about any connection between the celestial visitor and the late Julius Caesar, the populace of Rome immediately saw it as a symbol of Caesar's ascension to the gods as well as his approval of both the games in his honor and of his great-nephew Octavian. Octavian, for his part, seized upon the occurrence and helped push a measure through the Senate which granted Caesar divine status. He lost no time in putting up a large monument to Caesar in the temple of Venus, adorning its head with a star. Two years later, Octavian constructed a temple to the Divine Julius Caesar in the Roman forum. The temple, which was built upon the site of Caesar's cremation pyre, was also known as the "Temple of the Comet Star", the only temple in Rome dedicated to the cult of a comet. Coins of Julius Caesar minted immediately after his death bear the image of Caesar on the obverse face and an eight-pointed star on the reverse face with the words Diuus Iulius ("Divine Julius"). For the next two and one half decades, the comet star also appeared on all Augustan coinage, forever linking the comet's appearance and the divine nature of Julius Caesar to the personage of Octavian (Caesar Augustus).

During the period of shared control of the Empire between Marc Anthony and Octavian, Anthony began to consort with the Egyptian Queen Cleopatra, the last member of the Macedonian-Greek dynasty of Ptolemy. Anthony became so involved with Cleopatra that he effectively went into semi-retirement. Octavian illicitly obtained a copy of Anthony's will in which he stated that upon his death, all of his possessions were to be given to Cleopatra and his body was to be buried in Egypt. Romans had a great mistrust of Egypt and this was not the way a Roman ruler was expected to behave. Octavian used this to gather support against his co-ruler. In 31 B.C., the armies of the two men met at Actium in Greece, and after a great naval battle, Octavian emerged victorious. He chased Anthony to Egypt where first Anthony, and then Cleopatra, committed suicide. This left Octavian the sole ruler of the Roman Empire. Octavian went through the motions of handing power back to the Senate, but the Senate, knowing full well where the real power resided, handed it all back to Octavian who took the title Augustus and became the first Emperor of Rome. For the next century, his descendants would rule the Empire as the Julio-Claudian Dynasty.

Octavian's father had been a member of the Senate but it was through his grandmother, Julia, that he gained his ultimate connection to the path of Emperor. Julia was the sister of Julius Caesar and when Caesar had no male children of his own (there is a question of whether or not Cleopatra's son, Caesarion, was Caesar's child), he made his grandnephew, Octavian, his legal heir. Octavian served with Caesar in Spain in 46 A.D. when he was only 16 years old and was in Illyricum (modern Albania) waiting to join Caesar on a new campaign to Parthia (Persia) when he received the news of Caesar's assassination. The Roman historian Suetonius described Octavian (Augustus):

> *"He was unusually handsome and exceedingly graceful in all periods of his life, though he cared nothing for personal adornment. He was so far from being particular about the dressing of his hair, that he would have several barbers working in a hurry at the same time, and as far as for his beard he now had it clipped and now shaved, while at the same time he would either be reading or writing something."*

Augustus was keen to be seen as ushering in a new era for Rome so he spent much of his early career as Emperor repairing temples and building new public structures including the famous Pantheon. One building he did not construct was a palace for himself; instead he continued to live in a modest but spacious house on the Palatine Hill. He is remembered in the Bible as the Emperor that issued the great census that resulted in Joseph and Mary having to travel from Galilee to Bethlehem where Jesus was born (Luke 2:1). Augustus was not a great soldier but that does not mean that he did not care about the military successes of his army. In 9 A.D., Quintilius Varus, commander of the Legions on the German frontier along the Rhine River, was ambushed in a trap set by the Germans in the Teutoburg Forest. All three Legions (XVII, XVIII, and XIX) were completely destroyed and their eagle standards, touched by Augustus himself, were captured. Augustus was so stunned by this loss that it may have ultimately led to his death. It is recorded that for months afterwards, he went into a virtual state of mourning, neither shaving his beard nor cutting his hair. He was also seen from time to time hitting his head against a door and crying out "Quintilius Varus, give me back my Legions".

In later life, Augustus began to withdraw from public activity, citing old age and health issues. He also became more and more conservative, frequently chiding the members of his court and the Senate for living too lavishly. Augustus also promulgated a number of conservative laws which attempted to curb Roman vice, notably homosexuality. All of these new edicts were met with opposition from his peers and as soon as Augustus died in 14 A.D., most of his more conservative social laws were either changed or functionally ignored.

Augustus, like Caesar, had no male heirs. He did have two grandsons of whom he was very fond; so much so, that he adopted them as his sons and intended for them to be his heirs. However, both died before Augustus and he was forced to adopt his step-son Tiberius. Augustus' reign was longer and more successful than he or anyone else could have anticipated, lasting effectively for over 40 years (from 44 B.C. to 14 A.D.). Since almost two generations of Romans had not known any other leader, having someone from his lineage as his successor proved to be an easy and smooth process and Tiberius became Emperor in 14 A.D. with little to no opposition.

The Emperor Tiberius (14-37 A.D.) remains a somewhat enigmatic figure as some historians portray him as a blood thirsty and cruel tyrant while others point to a life of sexual depravity and degeneracy. It must be remembered that because of Augustus' long life, Tiberius did not assume the throne until he was 54 years of age; he retired from public life at the age of 67 and died at the age of 77. In his early life, Tiberius had been a soldier of some note having served in Syria against the Parthians, then in Gaul, and finally on the German frontier. By 6 B.C., he had had enough of military life and retired, only to return to active political life when Augustus designated him as his political heir. There are some indications that Tiberius never wanted to be Emperor but was gradually persuaded to come out of retirement for the good of Rome.

Much of Tiberius' active term as Emperor was influenced by a man named Sejanus, who was head of the Emperor's personal body guard, the Praetorian Guard. Sejanus was an extremely ambitious individual who is believed to have committed several murders of potential heirs to the throne in order to set himself up as a possible successor to Tiberius. Sejanus was also known to be strongly anti-Semitic. It is unknown for certain, but a number of scholars now believe that Pontius Pilate, a known friend of Sejanus, received his appointment as Procurator to Judea due to his mentor's closeness to the Emperor. If true, then Pontius Pilate may also have been influenced politically by Sejanus which could then explain Pilate's frequent attempts to aggravate the Jewish community during his 10 year term as Procurator of Judea.

Tiberius, returning to retirement from public life, placed more and more power under the control of Sejanus. In 31 A.D., Tiberius appointed Sejanus to the Senate. However, almost as soon as doing so, Tiberius seems to have had second thoughts about granting Sejanus so much control in his absence. He may have been forewarned of a plot to stage a coup d'état as shortly after appointing Sejanus to the Senate, Tiberius had him arrested and killed.

Tiberius was never the popular ruler that his predecessor Augustus had been. He was seen by the Senate as well as the populace as stiff and arrogant. Tiberius became increasingly unpopular over his refusal to host lavish games for the people's entertainment. His complete dislike for public life culminated in his retirement to the island of Capri. It is during his retreat to Capri that the Bible mentions the beginning of John the Baptist's ministry, "in the 15th year of the reign of Caesar Tiberius" (Luke 3:1-2). At the Imperial Residence on Capri, all excesses were allowed. Many stories of extreme cruelty and depravity have been written about the aging Emperor, most of which were written by political enemies so their truthfulness is questionable. Tiberius' villa on Capri was adjacent to a nearly 1,000 foot cliff from which he supposedly had those people he was tired of or displeased him thrown to their deaths in what became known as the Salto di Tiberio ("Tiberius Leap"). Tiberius is said to have enjoyed the company of young adolescent boys whom he liked to call his "minnows". Tiberius was very careful to control rumors of what went on in Capri and when he believed someone might talk about things the Emperor did not want disclosed, over the cliff and into the sea they went. One of those "minnows" who was invited to Capri was his grandnephew, Caligula. Caligula came to Capri in 31 A.D., and many thought that the young man would never survive his stay. But Caligula had a knack for acting and Tiberius grew to enjoy his company, even to the extent of formally adopting him as his grandson. Tiberius became seriously ill in 37 A.D., and died at the age of 77 while still at Capri. Historians to this day are uncertain if Tiberius finally died of natural causes or if he was smothered by a pillow held by Caligula. In either event, Caligula assumed the throne as the third Emperor of the Julio-Claudian Dynasty at age 24.

Gaius Julius Caesar Germanicus was descended from Julius Caesar through Tiberius. His father, Germanicus, was a famous and successful general and it is said that he took young Gaius at age 2 on a military campaign to Germany. The soldiers were so amused at the general's son dressed in his tiny military uniform that they nicknamed him Caligula ("little boots"), a diminutive form of the word for Roman army shoes, caligae. The nickname stuck and he was known as Caligula for the remainder of his life.

Caligula was a noble and moderate ruler for the first six months of his reign. He returned to Rome from Capri and was seen at the games and other public events, which endeared him to the masses. Caligula was perceived by the public to be a return to the days of Augustus in direct contrast to Tiberius' disdain for public spectacle. In the latter part of his first year as Emperor, Caligula became seriously ill, almost dying. He recovered, but the brush with death seems to have severely changed his personality. He appears to have suffered from both epilepsy as well as extreme insomnia, seldom sleeping more than three hours a night. Caligula's personality changed dramatically to one bent on cruelty, sadism and sexual promiscuity. He is reputed to have raped women in public and had his enemies beheaded in front of him while he ate dinner. He slept with the wives of prominent Roman men and then discussed his conquests in public, sometimes in front of the husbands he cuckolded. He is reported to have had an incestuous relationship with all three of his sisters, especially his favorite sister, Drusilla. When she died in 38 A.D., Caligula ordered her immediate deification and went into mourning for a period in Sicily.

Caligula was famous for his love of his favorite racehorse, Incitatus. The horse was kept in a marble stall with purple blankets and a special harness festooned with precious gems. He also built two immense ships to serve as lavish floating palaces on Lake Nemi. The lake was drained in the 1930's by Benito Mussolini and the remains of the ships and all their fabulous artifacts were recovered. So lavish was his lifestyle that he completely went through Tiberius' immense legacy in only two years. In order to raise money, Caligula instituted taxes on a number of institutions including marriage, divorce, lawsuits, prostitution and the like. He began to live like, and demanded to be treated as a living god. In the eastern part of the Empire he was readily deified. He even demanded that an immense statue of himself be placed in the Temple in Jerusalem. Large-scale unrest broke out in many places across Palestine and Syria because of this order, but he died before it could be carried out.

Caligula is not mentioned in the Bible but one of his associates and friends is. Caligula was great friends with Herod Agrippa I, the grandson of Herod the Great, and when he became Emperor, he had Herod Antipas banished to Gaul and placed Agrippa on the throne of Judea. This reinstitution of a King of Judea temporarily stopped the system of Roman Procurators, which was then re-established in 44 A.D. with Herod Agrippa's death.

In the latter part of Caligula's reign, his relationship with the Senate became extremely strained. Finally, several members of the Senate acted and in 41 A.D., Caligula was assassinated in much the same manner as his ancestor, Julius Caesar. It appears that the Senate believed with Caligula out of the way and no obvious successor, that they could restore the Roman Republic. They were surprised when the day after the assassination, the Praetorian Guard publicly named Caligula's uncle, Claudius, Emperor.

Claudius was the most unlikely choice for Emperor. To avoid the wrath of his crazed nephew, Claudius played the fool at court. Suetonius described Claudius in the following manner:

"He was tall but not slender, with an attractive face, becoming white hair, and a full neck. But when he walked, his weak knees gave way under him and he had many disagreeable traits. He would foam at the mouth and trickle at the nose; he stammered besides and his head was very shaky at all times."

He amused Caligula and thus Caligula let him live. When the senatorial conspirators struck Caligula down, the Praetorian Guard went on a rampage searching for and killing the conspirators and anyone else they could find who was suspected to have been part of the plot. One soldier, in searching the royal palace, saw a pair of feet sticking out from behind a curtain. He drew back the curtain, recognized Claudius, and fell down and proclaimed him Emperor.

Claudius was 50 years old when he became Emperor in 41 A.D. He had distinguished parents but despite his high birth, he lived in relative obscurity. His jerky movements, speech impediment and tendency to dribble (symptoms which seem to suggest he may have suffered from cerebral palsy), made him an embarrassment to his family and he was kept out of public eye. His mental faculties were not impaired and Claudius spent his life studying Roman and Etruscan history, even writing several books on the subject, none of which have survived. He also took refuge in other pursuits, mainly gambling and drinking. Claudius, by the time he became Emperor, may have been an alcoholic.

Claudius' reign has been criticized for allowing the major women in his life to dominate him. Messalina was Claudius' third wife, yet the first to bear him a son, Britannicus. Messalina saw her son as the logical heir to the throne and arranged to have all potential rivals and unwanted family members killed. Messalina was not only notorious for her killing of rivals to the throne but also for her adulteries. Her lovers ranged from leading senators to actors. Either Claudius did not know about her escapades or, more likely, he turned a blind eye. Pliny the Elder stated that Messalina even worked in a Roman brothel under the name "She-Wolf". She is famously said to have entered into a 24 hour contest with all the famous prostitutes in Rome, at the end of which she claimed victory with a score of 25 partners. While Claudius was away at Ostia, Messalina forced a high-ranking consul designate, Gaius Silius, to divorce his wife and marry Messalina in front of witnesses. It is unclear what Messalina hoped to accomplish by this affront to the Emperor, but on his return to Rome, Claudius had both Silius and Messalina arrested and executed.

Claudius had no intention of ever marrying again but was eventually persuaded to marry Caligula's surviving sister, Agrippina. Claudius married Agrippina in 49 A.D., with special dispensation from the Senate as she was his niece. Agrippina proved to be as scheming as Messalina; her main objective was to ensure that her son from a previous marriage would be placed ahead of Britannicus (the son of Claudius and Messalina). In 50 A.D., she had Claudius formally adopt Lucius Domitius Ahenobarbus as his son, who then took the adopted name of "Nero". Nero was soon promoted ahead of Britannicus and made the heir apparent. In 53 A.D., Agrippina also arranged for Nero to marry Claudius' daughter Octavia. Claudius by this time was already gravely ill but Agrippina could not afford to wait for him to die of natural causes.

She enlisted the help of an expert poisoner and Claudius was dispatched to his ancestors on the night of October 12-13, 54 A.D., leaving his stepson Nero to succeed him.

Claudius is mentioned briefly in the Bible, the most notable being in Acts 18:2 where he is said to have expelled the Jews from Rome. This is believed to have occurred around 49 A.D., and is also referred to by the Roman historian, Suetonius:

> *"Since the Jews constantly made disturbances at the instigation of Chrestus, he [the Emperor Claudius] expelled them from Rome."*

It is interesting to note that, at least at this time, the Romans made no distinction between the Jews and the early Christians as "Chrestus" clearly refers to Christ. Other than this one expulsion, Claudius is not known to have been a persecutor of the Christians as were Nero and Domitian later.

Nero is the one Roman Emperor that everyone, regardless of their knowledge of history, has heard of. In film, he is always portrayed as a monster, living a luxurious lifestyle while his subjects are treated poorly and his enemies are tortured and killed in gruesome ways. The historical Nero is a bit more complex than that. Nero was 16 years old when Claudius died. Despite his relatively young age and the fact that he was not Claudius' blood relative, he was almost universally supported by the Praetorian Guard, the army and the Senate. During the first five years of his reign, Nero seemed to justify that support. In the early part of his reign he made a speech before the Senate in which he promised to grant the Senate a greater role in the government. He made a huge donation to the support of the Praetorian Guard and he was generally well regarded by the people.

Nero came to the throne because his mother, Agrippina, was the sister of Caligula and the last wife of the Emperor Claudius. Yet there was still the problem of Britannicus, Claudius' biological son. Nero saw Britannicus as a very real rival so on the night of February 11, 55 A.D., less than four months after his father died, Britannicus was poisoned. When he collapsed at the dinner table, Nero claimed that Britannicus was having a seizure and had him carried to his bedroom where he expired without any interference or help from a doctor. The body was secretly carried out the next day and hastily buried.

The next problem was his mother, Agrippina, who sought to rule through her son. In 59 A.D., Nero invited her to dine with him at a coastal estate in Baiae. For the return trip, he put her aboard a specially designed boat. Part way through the voyage, the lead-filled canopy over her chair collapsed and she was saved from being crushed only by the height of the furniture's arms. Next, the boat was capsized on purpose, but somehow Agrippina was able to swim to shore and make it to one of her villas. Finally, soldiers were sent to dispatch her.

While working on how to eliminate his mother, Nero fell in love with a woman of great beauty named Poppaea Sabina. She was married to Marcus Otho, one of his closest friends, but that did not hinder Nero from making her his lover. The problem was that Nero was still married to Claudius' daughter Octavia. Only in 62 A.D. did he feel secure enough from the Senate that he was able to divorce Octavia and marry Poppaea. She bore him a daughter that died several months after birth. When she became pregnant again, Nero, in a fit of temper, kicked her in the stomach and both Poppaea and the baby died.

Nero was known as a great patron of the arts. He became quite skilled at playing the harp and enjoyed playing and singing in various venues in Italy as well as in Greece. While performances from a minstrel or an actor were enjoyed by the patrician class, the profession itself was considered very lowly and not something that a person of quality in Roman life, let alone the Emperor, should engage in. Nero was oblivious to the Senators' scorn but his reputation amongst the elite of Roman was damaged. In 64 A.D., a great fire broke out which ravaged Rome and further damaged the Emperor's reputation, this time with the average citizen. The fire broke out in the region of the Circus Maximus and spread through 10 of the city's 14 regions. Despite the fact that Nero, who was away at the time, rushed back to his capital and did everything he could to organize relief measures, he was not only blamed for the disaster, but many Romans believed he had set the fire on purpose. This belief stemmed from the fact that shortly afterwards, Nero appropriated 300 acres of the best land in the center of Rome that had been cleared by the fire and built a lavish palace for himself known as the Domus Aurea (Golden House). The house had a colossal 120 foot high statue of the Emperor. Contemporaries regarded the waste of space and lavish spending on the Golden House as a crime. To try and deflect attention away from himself, Nero blamed the fire on the new emerging sect of Christians:

"Nero substituted as culprits, and punished with the utmost refinements of cruelty, a class of men, loathed for their vices, whom the crowd styled as Christians. Vast numbers were convicted, not so much on the count of arson as for hatred of the human race. And derision accompanied their end; they were covered with wild beasts' skins and torn to death by dogs; or they were fastened on crosses, and when daylight failed were burned to serve as lamps by night."
Tacitus Annals XV.44

Nero is alluded to in the Bible (Acts 25:11; Philippians 1:12; 4:22) but never actually mentioned by name. He is believed to have been the Emperor who judged and condemned Paul, and later Peter, to death. It is believed that Paul was executed by way of beheading as he was a Roman citizen and could not be crucified as Peter was.

Nero's lavish spending largely bankrupted the State, so he increasingly raised taxes on virtually everything, which did not further endear him further to the public. A revolt broke out in Spain in 68 A.D., which gathered support among the Senate and also the Praetorian Guard. Nero tried to escape to the sea but receiving no help from his guards, he retreated back to his palace. He was found hiding in one of the back rooms when the soldiers came to arrest him. Nero cried out, "What an artist the world is losing" and then stabbed himself in the neck and died. He was just 30 years old.

The death of Nero left a huge vacuum of power in the Empire as there was no heir. The Julio-Claudian Dynasty was finally over after 95 years of rule. The army put forth candidates from every part of the Empire: in the west from Spain was General Galba; in the north from Germania the army supported Vitellius; Marcus Otho, close friend of Nero, saw himself as a contender and was supported by the armies in Italy; and finally, General Vespasian had the support of the armies in the eastern part of the Empire.

Galba reached Rome first in mid-68 A.D. and was proclaimed Emperor by the Senate. He was already 70 years old and was seen by most as just a stop-gap selection to forestall any additional revolts around the Empire. Galba refused to pay any tribute to the army for supporting him, saying that he was used to imposing levies on troops, not buying them. Thus, when the forces of Otho marched on Rome in early 69 A.D., Galba was stabbed to death by one of his own soldiers and Otho was proclaimed the new Emperor. Many members of the Roman Senate did not trust Otho because of his close friendship with Nero so, when Vitellius and the armies from the north arrived in Rome, Otho found he had no real support. He quietly retired to his room and committed suicide. Vitellius was then proclaimed Emperor, the third such proclamation in less than a year.

While all this unrest was unfolding in Rome, the armies in the east proclaimed that their general, Vespasian, should be Emperor. At first, Vespasian balked at the idea but was quickly convinced that he was indeed in position to save Rome from disaster. His army fought their way into Rome on December 20, 69 A.D. His troops found Vitellius in his home, dragged him to the forum where he was tortured and killed, and his body thrown into the Tiber River. Vespasian was proclaimed Emperor which signaled the start of a new line of Emperors known as the Flavian Dynasty after Vespasian's family name.

Vespasian was a completely new kind of Emperor, middle class (not patrician), and a man with real-life experience in almost every part of the Empire. He had served as a military tribune in Thrace (modern Bulgaria) and later in Crete and Cyrene (North Africa). He had commanded the 2nd Legion (Augusta) in the conquest of Britain in 43-47 A.D., then served as Governor of North Africa. Nero had placed him in charge of all the armies participating in the Jewish War (66-70 A.D.) and he was in the process of initiating the siege of Jerusalem when he was called to march on Rome. Vespasian left his eldest son Titus in charge of the army when he left for Rome.

Vespasian was considered by most scholars to be one of, if not the best Emperor of first century A.D. Rome. His conscientious attention to the welfare of the general populace of both Rome and the provinces won him widespread support. The Roman historian Tacitus wrote that "He, unlike all his predecessors, was the only Emperor that was changed for the better by his office". Vespasian did not build a palace for himself, but rather lived in a house full of gardens on the northern side of the city. He also did not travel far from Rome during his 10 years as Emperor and was always available to address any pressing problems of the Empire. According to Suetonius, Vespasian had a strict routine which he maintained every day. He would arise before dawn and spend the first half of the day meeting with senators and officials and reading reports on the activities of the Empire. He would then have a drive through the city with his wife, and after her death, with one of his concubines. This was followed by a nap and then a visit to the baths. He ended the day with dinner, usually with friends and/or officials, where the business of the Empire would be discussed further.

Vespasian found the treasury of the Empire severely depleted after the abuses of Nero. He declared that the sum of 40 thousand million sesterces was needed to regain financial stability (Roman officials always quoted large sums in thousands of millions). To restock the Government coffers, Vespasian imposed a wide range of taxes, including increases on traditional taxes and the institution of new taxes. One of his most infamous new taxes was the imposition of a levy on the use of public latrines. When his son Titus objected that such a levy was beneath the dignity of the Emperor, Vespasian was reported to have held up a handful of golden coins and said, "See, my son, if they have any smell". Vespasian was also not above selling lower ranking public offices.

Titus concluded the Jewish War in 70 A.D. with the complete sacking of Jerusalem including the destruction of Herod's Temple. With this victory came a huge amount of wealth which Vespasian used to build his greatest contribution to Rome, the Vespasian Amphitheater, better known as the Colosseum because it was built on the site near Nero's colossal statue to himself. Archeologists exploring the outer entrance ways of the Colosseum have found a series of holes which appear to have corresponded to bronze letters that once were present over the portals. As examples of Roman bronze letters are known, the location of the holes can be assigned to specific letters. Reconstructing the message indicates that the famous Roman Colosseum was not only built by the treasures gained from the Temple in Jerusalem, but some of the building itself was done by Jewish slave labor.

Vespasian died in 79 A.D. after a sudden and brief illness. The succession had long since been established as Titus was mentioned no fewer than 14 times in Roman records as the heir apparent. Titus, who ruled for only two years, from 79-81 A.D., is a bit of a historical enigma. He served in the army as a young man, first in Britain and Germany, and then as commander of a Legion (Apollinaris) under his father in the Jewish War. He assumed command of the eastern army when his father marched on Rome, and concluded the Jewish War with the successful siege and destruction of Jerusalem in 70 A.D. While he was seen as his father's constant helper and protector, it was his passion for the Jewish Queen Berenice that brought him the most scorn. Berenice was the sister, lover and queen to Herod Agrippa II (Acts 25:13, 23; 26:30). Apparently Titus fell in love with her during the Jewish War but eastern monarchs were so disliked by the Romans that he did not invite her to Rome until 75 A.D. She lived openly with the Emperor-to-be, but such was her unpopularity that he had to send her back to Judea.

Titus continued his father's policy of compassion for the subjects of the Empire. He is recorded to have said to dinner guests one evening that he had not done anything for anyone that day and thus he considered it to have been a "lost day". This attitude of compassion for the populace was best demonstrated when the twin cities of Pompeii and Herculaneum were destroyed by the eruption of Mount Vesuvius in 79 A.D. Titus poured disaster relief into the area and visited the region twice to make sure that the people affected by the disaster were being treated well.

Titus' end came suddenly and completely unexpectedly. While journeying from Rome to the family's hill country estate, he came down with severe fever and chills, probably the result of malaria. Within a few days, Titus was dead at the age of 42. His dying words were "I have made but one mistake". Nobody knows what he meant by these enigmatic words but it may have had to do with his younger brother, Domitian. There has been a great deal of speculation that Domitian had something to do with Titus' death. After Titus became ill but before he died, Domitian sped back to Rome in order to assume the throne. Titus and Domitian had never had a warm relationship and there is no indication that Domitian was ever in line for the succession. However, Titus died childless and the Praetorian Guard proclaimed Domitian Emperor the day after Titus' death.

Domitian saw the role of Emperor as one of an autocratic monarch with absolute power. He was not as handsome as Titus and he went bald in early middle age. Portraits of the Emperor however, always show him with flowing locks and curled hair. Despite his personal vanity, he appears to have been an able administrator and he did not neglect the needs of the Empire. He attempted to raise the standards of public morality, passing laws forbidding the castration of any male and meting out punishment to any senator or public official who was caught practicing homosexuality. Domitian was not the soldier his brother or his father had been, but that did not stop him from embarking on a campaign in Germany and awarding himself the title "Germanicus" after a minor victory. He also won victories over the Dacians in what is now modern day Romania.

Domitian was not a happy individual and he suffered from a severe sense of inadequacy. He was also a fearful man, always afraid that someone in the Empire was going to kill him. His paranoia began to take hold of his entire life and he had his palace festooned with polished marble and mirrors so he could see if anyone was plotting against him. He turned against the Senate, having many of its members arrested, tortured and put to death for supposed treason. His reign of terror actually served to work against him as members of his family and the royal household became so fearful for their lives that they ultimately collaborated to kill the Emperor. The Royal Chamberlain struck first and then was joined by all the members of the family who hacked him to death. Domitian had no male heirs so the Senate viewed his death as an opportunity to regain control and placed one of its older members, Nerva, on the throne, ending the Flavian Dynasty after a relatively short period of 27 years (69-96 A.D.).

While Hollywood typically portrays Nero as the great antagonist of the Christians, it was actually Domitian who was the greatest persecutor of the early Christian faith. The Emperor Domitian perceived Christianity as a direct threat to the Empire and had many Christians crucified, imprisoned or exiled. The best known exile of this period was the Apostle John, who was sent to the island of Patmos to work in the mines (Revelation 1). God, however, not only spared the apostle's life, but used John's exile to give him His final vision which comes down to us in the last book of the New Testament, Revelation.

The city of Rome was unquestionably the center of the known world during the first century A.D. Historians variously estimate the total population at between 800,000 and 1,200,000, of which as much as 50-60 percent were slaves. Roman society was almost entirely dependent on slaves, and contrary to the common portrayal in movies, slaves were highly prized and generally well-treated. This was especially true of household slaves who not only helped with all the chores around the house but took care of the owner's children as well. Educated Greek slaves were typically employed as tutors for the children not yet of school age. This does not mean that some slaves were not ill-treated. Captured enemy soldiers, criminals or those deemed a danger to the Empire would be sent to work in the mines. Life there was brutal and usually short. Slaves either wore a collar or a tag of ownership. These could be removed if the owner decided to free a slave but a freed slave needed to have a document of manumission to prove to the authorities that he was indeed a freed man.

Romans lived either in a house (*domus*) or an apartment complex (*insula*). Typical Roman houses were styled after Etruscan homes and built as a series of inward facing rooms around a central courtyard or atrium – the latter having either a fountain or a garden. Houses typically had several bedrooms (*cubicula*) which were often quite small and only used for sleeping; a *tablinium* (library), where family records were kept as well as portraits of ancestors (ancestors were revered); a *triclinium* or dining room as well as a kitchen and a lavatory. Houses usually had only a single door which faced the main street. Windows were rare and houses seldom had more than a few, also usually facing the main street. Well-to-do Romans may also have owned a villa in the countryside or near the ocean. Such villas were designed for rest and pleasure and frequently contained a bath or a swimming pool. Many Romans decorated the walls of their homes with painted murals or mosaics. Country villas and resort towns, such as Pompeii, were especially rich in such decoration. Many Roman house murals contained scenes of either people or gods engaging in sexual activity. The Romans saw sex as one of the pleasures of life and depictions were not considered pornographic. Houses, and especially country villas, used a great deal of terracotta tiles and bricks, both for roofing as well as flooring and walkways. As a result, such bricks and tiles were mass produced and could be found all across the Empire.

Roman clothing was typically simple; men wore a tunic which was like a long t-shirt that was tightened at the waist by a belt. Both men and women wore an undergarment called an indutus which could either be a loincloth or a leather bikini-like garment. Tunics were always short sleeved; long-sleeved garments, especially for men, were considered effeminate. A toga would generally be worn over the tunic, especially when outside the house. Togas were made from a single piece of cloth, typically about 18 feet in length and 7 feet in width which could be wrapped and folded around the body in several styles. Togas were very much a status symbol and their color and decoration were meant to distinguish social classes. Togas were also expensive and required frequent cleaning, adding to their cost. In cold or inclement weather, a cape or cloak could be worn as an outer garment.

Women also wore tunics around the house but when going outside, women, especially those who were married, wore a one-piece full length dress called a stola. The stola would be gathered at the waist by a wide belt. The stola, like the toga, was a symbol of wealth and social class could be determined by the fabric and colors used. Women wore a shawl or palla if the weather was cold.

Beards were not popular and men either kept them well-trimmed or were clean shaven and consequently there were many barbers in Rome. Women spent a great deal of time arranging their hair in layers and in curls. Wigs were also very fashionable among women and blonde German wigs or jet-black wigs from India were the fashion rage in Rome during the first century A.D.

As with all Roman cities, the center of activity in Rome was the forum. Fortunately for us today, the Italian government has cleared more than 50 vertical feet of rubbish that had been

Figure 134. Via Sacra Leading into the Roman Forum. (Photo Courtesy of Louis Aulbach and Linda Gorski)

laid down over the last 2,000 years to return the ruins in and around the forum to the ground level of Paul's day. The Appian Way entered the city from the southeast. Past the great hippodrome, the Circus Maximus, the road entered the forum through the Via Sacra, the "Sacred Way" (Figure 134). This was the path leading up to the Capitoline Hill that all triumphal returning Roman armies took. When Paul arrived in the spring of 60 A.D., the Arch of Titus (see Figure 134) which celebrated Rome's victory over the Jews and the destruction of Jerusalem, had yet to be built. However, Paul would have seen the immense size of the Roman forum which was surrounded by temples to various gods and goddesses as well as the administrative buildings which housed the Senate (the *Curia*) and other municipal functions (Figures

Figure 135. The Via Sacra Looking East Towards the Colosseum. (Photo Courtesy of Louis Aulbach and Linda Gorski)

Figure 136. The Old Forum in Rome Looking West. (Photo Courtesy of Louis Aulbach and Linda Gorski)

Figure 137. Detail of the Old Forum at Rome.

135-138). While the Colosseum (see Figure 135) also had not yet been built, the sheer size of the central part of Rome must have nonetheless been very impressive to Paul and his companions.

Shops of every type were everywhere in Rome (Figure 139). People could buy everything in a Roman market from food to pottery to clothing. Since there was no refrigeration, food was purchased almost daily. The

Figure 138. Remains of the Temple to Pollux and Castor, Forum, Rome.

average Roman diet was largely based on bread. As a consequence, bakeries were the single most common shop in Rome and the streets would be filled with the smell of fresh baked bread every morning. Romans typically ate only one large meal a day, at mid-day (cena). Breakfast was typically bread, perhaps accompanied by some cheese or honey. The mid-day meal would consist of a stew or soup with bread and vegetables. Bread would be sweetened or flavored with honey or cheese and eaten along with sausage, chicken, fish or oysters. Vegetables such as cabbage, beans, lentils, onions, lettuce, garlic and parsnips were commonly available. Meat was not common except for the very wealthy. If people lived near the coast, fish and shellfish could be added to the diet. To provide meat for the general population, the Romans introduced the commercial raising and eating of chicken. Chickens do not take up much space and they can be grown from egg to full-size fryer in less than 40 days. Chickens often accompanied the army and many Roman house

Figure 139. Shops Lining the Forum in Rome.

murals and mosaics depict chickens or roosters. Dinner was usually a light meal unless the family was giving a dinner party. Dinners with guests were special events and the hosts typically went all out to impress their guests with their wealth. Special delicacies including foods from all over the Empire would be served, which not only emphasized the host's wealth and status but reinforced the fact that Rome was the one great power in the world. Special meals could include such delicacies as stuffed dormice, an abundance of oysters, eels or caviar, and birds or meats that were stuffed in multiple layers (think "Turducken"). Romans loved wine but drank it diluted and heated and spiced; drinking undiluted raw wine was considered barbaric. Only nursing babies drank milk. Drinking animal milk was also considered barbaric so milk was used primarily for making cheese and various medicines. The Romans cut their food with a knife but generally ate almost all of the meals with their hands.

Just as important as the food the guests were served was the tableware on which the food was served and eaten. Prior to the first century A.D., common people ate their meals on very plain, buff to terracotta-colored tableware. A much fancier form of tableware, known as Terra Sigillata or Samian Ware, was being made but was generally priced above what the average

Roman citizen could afford. The Emperor Augustus decreed that Terra Sigillata should be mass produced in order to make the finer ware affordable to all citizens. Production centers in Italy (Arretium) and Gaul began to produce Terra Sigillata ware in huge quantities, which were then shipped all over the Empire. Terra Sigillata ware is characterized by a glossy red-orange slip and a high degree of burnishment (polish). Common Terra Sigillata can be found in almost every Roman site from the first century A.D., from Palestine and Syria to North Africa to all across Europe. More lavish versions contained molded reliefs of animals, gods or goddesses along the rim.

Other common Roman ceramic vessels included large, elongate storage vessels known as amphorae (singular, amphora). A Roman amphora typically held just under 26 liters of liquid, most commonly wine or olive oil and sometimes pickled fish. The Romans believed that an amphora was no longer useful if it had contained olive oil or fish packed in olive oil because the oil and its smell permeated all the pores of the vessel. Therefore they were not recycled but merely thrown onto a large rubbish pile. In Rome today there is a hill called Monte Testaccio which covers nearly a square kilometer and is 115 feet in height. The mound is purely artificial and is composed of nothing but broken and discarded Roman pottery vessels, mainly amphorae, with an estimated 25 million pottery sherds. Roman sites from the first century A.D. frequently contain in excess of several million pottery sherds and of these, 50-80 percent will come from amphorae. Other common ceramic vessels included thick storage jars (dolla or pithos), buff to terracotta-colored cooking pots, and thick vessels called mortaria which were used for grinding and processing foods.

While many average citizens still drank from cups made of pottery, the fastest growing fad was the use of glassware, fueled by innovations in the production of glass. Glass manufacture had been known as far back as the eighth century B.C., but the Romans developed a new process using sodium carbonate which allowed the glass to be blown, opening up an almost unlimited variety of shapes and forms. The most common glass vessels were drinking cups and small bottles to hold special oils or perfumes.

Roman citizens, especially those living in the capital, enjoyed spectacular entertainment. Games in arenas, or later in the Colosseum (Flavian Amphitheater) as well as chariot races in the Circus Maximus, were always popular attractions. Many productions in the arena would recreate famous historical battles or mythological adventures. Stories about Hercules was very popular as were contests between gladiators and various imported wild animals. Some arenas could even be filled with a few feet of water in order to stage naval battles for the people's entertainment.

The most common form of entertainment that Roman citizens enjoyed was the bath. Baths were typically segregated between the classes but the Emperors provided many public baths that the average citizen could enjoy. Roman baths were not just baths but a combination of baths, gymnasiums or exercise clubs, and swimming pools. A Roman bath was a drawn-out process involving up to seven steps. First, oil would be rubbed into the skin. This would be followed by some exercise. After exercising, the bathers would retire to a hot room, essentially equivalent to a modern sauna. Men would discuss politics or the problems of the day while women would discuss their families in their own hot baths. Next came a swim in a thermally heated pool, during which time men in particular would drink wine and play board games. Games of chance involving dice were particularly popular throughout all classes of Roman society, up to and including the Emperor. Sometime during the hot bath, slaves would take specially designed bronze scrapers (*strigil*) and scrape the bathers' skins to remove the sweat and oil. The sweat of gladiators would often be collected and saved in glass vials for later resale. Many Roman women believed that gladiator sweat was a powerful aphrodisiac and perfume and it was highly prized, especially if it came from a champion gladiator. Lastly came a quick dip in a cold pool followed by a massage. Romans typically arose early in the day and worked until mid-day or early afternoon. Most of the afternoon was reserved for baths and relaxation to be followed by a family meal and then bed.

The Romans, like most ancient peoples, worshiped a large pantheon of gods and goddesses. Many of these deities were taken from the Greeks and Romanized. The Romans also adopted a number of foreign gods and allowed worship of these deities alongside their traditional gods and goddesses; Isis from Egypt and Artemis from Asia Minor are notable examples of this practice. Generally the Romans practiced religious tolerance as long as people were loyal to the Empire and paid their taxes. Judaism, while considered strange to the Romans due to its monotheism and moralistic laws, was generally tolerated across the Empire. The expulsion of the Jews from Rome in 49 A.D. was due to the "continued radical worship of Chrestos", according to Suetonius. The Romans feared Christianity because of its preaching of a kingdom greater than Rome, the Kingdom of Heaven, and that all people are equal and free under God. This was considered a direct threat to the institution of slavery and thus a direct threat to Rome's economy which was built upon slavery. However, after Claudius' death in 54 A.D., the new Emperor Nero allowed Jews (and Christians) to re-enter Rome. Thus, when Paul arrived in ca. 60 A.D., there were not only Jewish synagogues but a fledgling Christian church as well.

By the first century A.D., most Roman males of the patrician / senatorial class did not really believe in any of the gods. As such, religious practices were largely just for show for the masses. Most working class Romans may have believed in a god that oversaw or protected his particular profession. This is akin to, and may actually be the origin of, the modern practice of having a Patron Saint. Women were the most ardent believers in the deities, especially in goddesses that protected fertility, motherhood, children and the home. The cults of Artemis (Diana) and Venus (Aphrodite) were very popular throughout the Empire, particularly in Greece and Asia Minor. There were also large cults to Bacchus (Dionysus) as well as to Voluptas (pleasure); cults to the Emperor also became common throughout the first century A.D., especially in Asia but also in Rome as well.

The Romans had a fair system of justice in place including a number of legal rights for both the accused and the accuser. That does not mean that there weren't corrupt officials in the judicial system but by and large, the Roman legal system worked well. Upper class citizens got a jury trial with up to 80 sitting jurors. People would hire lawyers who were skilled orators who tried to persuade the jury of the merits of their case. Frequently, up-and-coming politicians would work as trial lawyers as a means to practice their oratory skills in public. There was no deliberation after the end of a trial; the jury would be asked to vote and the majority decision ruled.

Roman prisons were not designed for long-term incarceration. They were generally holding cells to be used for the time between the trial and sentencing and were typically used for major offenders who were thought to be flight threats. For the lower classes, penalties for minor offenses such as theft could be a monetary fine or a sentence of being beaten with lashes or rods, while major crimes were punishable by death. For major crimes, the wealthy could choose self-imposed exile as their punishment. By law, Roman citizens could not be put to death using crucifixion. Beheading was the most common form of execution, which is the way that tradition states that the Apostle Paul was executed. However, people could also be killed by being set on fire, dying in combat in the arena or choosing to work in the mines. Some criminals, such as those working life sentences in the mines, could later be sold to die in the arena. Crucifixion was reserved for use on non-Roman citizens of the Empire and was not just a manner of execution but was specifically designed to inflict the maximum amount of torture on the human body before death in order to demonstrate Roman power and bring terror to the population. Specific long square nails were used to pin the individual to the cross. Only after the victim had suffered for several hours would his legs be broken and he be allowed to collapse and then suffocate to death. This is why, when the soldiers found that Christ was already dead, they thrust the spear into his heart cavity to make sure that he wasn't shamming and was truly dead (John 19:34).

As soon as Paul arrived in Rome, he arranged for a meeting at his residence with the leaders of the local synagogue to see if they had received any messages about him from the Jewish leaders in Jerusalem. When they said they had not receive any such messages, Paul then used the gathering to preach the Gospel as he had done throughout Syria and Cilicia, Asia Minor, Greece and the islands of Rhodes, Crete and Malta:

"Three days later he called together the local Jewish leaders. When they had assembled, Paul said to them: 'My brothers, although I have done nothing against our people or against the customs of our ancestors, I was arrested in Jerusalem and handed over to the Romans. They examined me and wanted to release me, because I was not guilty of any crime deserving death. The Jews objected, so I was compelled to make an appeal to Caesar. I certainly did not intend to bring any charge against my own people. For this reason I have asked to see you and talk with you. It is because of the hope of Israel that I am bound with this chain.' They replied, 'We have not received any letters from Judea concerning you, and none of our people who have come from there has reported or said anything bad about you. But we want to hear what your views are, for we know that people everywhere are talking against this sect.' They arranged to meet Paul on a certain day, and came in even larger numbers to the place where he was staying. He witnessed to them from morning till evening, explaining about the kingdom of God, and from the Law of Moses and from the

Prophets he tried to persuade them about Jesus. Some were convinced by what he said, but others would not believe. They disagreed among themselves and began to leave after Paul had made this final statement: 'The Holy Spirit spoke the truth to your ancestors when he said through Isaiah the prophet:

'Go to this people and say,
You will be ever hearing but never understanding;
you will be ever seeing but never perceiving.'
For this people's heart has become calloused;
they hardly hear with their ears,
and they have closed their eyes.
Otherwise they might see with their eyes,
hear with their ears,
understand with their hearts
and turn, and I would heal them.'

Therefore I want you to know that God's salvation has been sent to the Gentiles, and they will listen!" (Acts 28:17-29)

As before, Paul used his extensive knowledge of the scriptures to show that Jesus was indeed the Messiah and the fulfillment of the Law and the Prophets. Some of the people listening believed and were converted to the Christian faith; however, others could not reconcile their Jewish beliefs with those of Jesus' Gospel. When Paul quoted the Prophet Isaiah saying that there will be people who will hear but not understand because their hearts are not open to the word of God, many of the Jews then left. And, as before, Paul said that God's salvation is for everyone and if the Jews in Rome will not listen, then the Gentiles will.

For Luke, this last scene in Rome epitomizes Paul's life as a missionary for the Gospel – the learned Jewish teacher, frequently rejected by his own people, was now the apostle to the Gentiles. Luke ends his narrative of Paul's journeys in Acts with two simple sentences:

"For two whole years Paul stayed there in his own rented house and welcomed all who came to see him. He proclaimed the kingdom of God and taught about the Lord Jesus Christ with all boldness and without hindrance!" (Acts 28:30-31)

So the question has to be asked: why did Luke stop here and not finish the story of the Apostle Paul? Instead, Luke leaves us with a string of open-ended questions. Why had Paul's interview with the Emperor not happened after two years? Did Paul ever stand trial in front of Caesar? Was he acquitted and released from Rome as some scholars believe? Was he re-incarcerated at a later date and then executed? How did Paul ultimately meet his end? Did Luke and his readers know the answers and the author was simply sparing us the sad details? Countless scholars, more learned than I, have written thousands of pages trying to answer these questions. However, I will give you some possible answers to these questions.

Figure 140. Bust of the Emperor Nero.

Paul and Luke arrived in Rome in the spring of 60 A.D. Paul was nearly 60 years old and for the last twenty plus years had lived a hard life of travel and physical hardships. He had been nearly stoned to death in Lystra; he had been severely beaten and imprisoned in Philippi; he had had physical confrontations in Corinth, Ephesus and Jerusalem. He spent two years in a Roman prison in Caesarea and had been shipwrecked and nearly drowned in a violent storm in the Mediterranean. He suffered from at least one severe malady and possibly more. When Paul arrived in Rome, he must have been a tired man, aged beyond his years.

Prior to Nero's ascension to the throne of the Empire, the Roman judicial system was experiencing a severe backlog of cases awaiting judgment. Nero promised to speed up the trial process by hearing major cases himself, and in the early years of his rule, he was successful. However, by 60 A.D., Nero had become less rational and his desire to listen to complex criminal cases was waning. He only heard cases now and then, and only largely only on a whim if the details of the case interested him (Figure 140). So the fact that Paul's case had not been heard by 62-63 A.D. is not surprising.

There are a number of traditions that say Paul was acquitted or received a temporary pardon and then conducted a Fourth Missionary Journey, traveling to Spain (believed to be "Tarshish") and then back to Greece before being re-arrested on some charge either in Greece or Troas and transported back to Rome for a second and final trial. Evidence that such a Fourth Missionary Journey took place is thin at best, and largely based on local traditions that date from well after the Apostle's life, possibly based on a desire to be part of the Paul story. Other early Christian scholars seeking to define a time when Paul could have written all of his epistles, needed another missionary journey in order to provide enough time for the Apostle to pen all his writings. Paul, in his letter to the Romans, had also mentioned his desire to someday visit Spain (Romans 15:24). However, we must remember that Paul was very insistent upon going to Rome to appeal his case before Caesar and was fully prepared to be martyred there if need be; remember the Apostle's final words to the Ephesian elders that he was heading to Jerusalem and would never see them again. In his letter to the Philippians, which may one of Paul's last letters, he speaks of his desire to die and "be with Christ" (Philippians 1:23). Paul was very determined to reach his final goal (*terma*) and I personally believe that this was Rome.

Christian tradition is that Paul was martyred before Peter. The time of Peter's death is unknown as well, but many scholars place it toward the end of Nero's rule, somewhere around 67 A.D. So in all likelihood, Paul was eventually given an audience with the Emperor, however brief, sometime after 62 A.D. The Jewish-Roman historian Josephus tells us that the Jewish leaders took advantage of the departure of the Procurator Festus in 62 A.D. to bring charges and have James, the brother of Jesus and leader of the church in Jerusalem, killed. These same Jewish leaders may have sent word to Rome or even traveled there themselves to press charges against Paul. Most certainly Paul would not have had many friends in his hearing before

Figure 141. Part of the Pillar where Paul was Bound and Executed. (Photo Courtesy of Louis Aulbach and Linda Gorski)

Nero. And, if the trial occurred after the great fire of 64 A.D., he would have had even fewer allies as Nero was looking for a scapegoat to blame for the disaster and the odd sect of Christians was the one that ultimately received the blame. Paul would have undoubtedly proclaimed Jesus Christ as the Lord of the world and spoken of the coming of God's Kingdom (Philippians 2:10-11). This would likely have been enough for Nero to condemn Paul to death.

Figure 142. *Basilica of the Church of St. Paul Outside the Walls. (Photo Courtesy of Louis Aulbach and Linda Gorski)*

As a Roman citizen, Paul could not have been crucified. Paul would have been led outside the city and executed. Christian tradition is that Paul was led out the southwestern gate of the city on the road to the port of Ostia (the Ostian Way). The apocryphal book, The Acts of Peter and Paul, written in the fourth century A.D., states that Paul was executed by beheading near the third milestone of the Ostian Way. Legend says that Paul was chained to a stone pillar and beheaded. His head reportedly bounced three times and each time, a fountain sprang up. The site is commemorated today by the Church of St. Paul at the Three Fountains (Tre Fontane). The current church was built in the sixteenth century over an original church from the fifth

Figure 143. *Replica of the Apostle Paul's Tombstone, Museum of the Ostian Way. (Photo Courtesy of Louis Aulbach and Linda Gorski)*

century. Inside the church is part of the pillar that Paul was reportedly chained to (Figure 141).

Another tradition places the spot of Paul's execution and burial one mile closer to the city at the site now marked by the immense Church of St. Paul Outside the Walls (Figure 142). Yet another Christian tradition dated from the second century A.D. says that Paul was not only executed there but also was buried there. The Emperor Constantine had a church built over the site and a larger one was built in 390 A.D. by the Emperor Theodosius. The current basilica was built in the 1800's after a fire destroyed the original structure.

At the heart of the basilica is a tombstone which reads "PAULO APOSTOLO MART" (Paul, Apostle and Martyr) (Figure 143). In 2006, Vatican officials discovered a marble sarcophagus underneath the tombstone. A tiny hole was drilled into the sarcophagus and it was found to contain purple cloth lined with gold, a blue linen cloth, and

Figure 144. Sarcophagus of the Apostle Paul, Basilica St. Paul Outside the Walls. (Photo Courtesy of Louis Aulbach and Linda Gorski)

the remnants of a red-colored incense. Bone fragments could be seen and a few tiny particles were removed and subjected to radiocarbon analysis. The results indicated that the bones dated from either the first or second century A.D. In 2009, Pope Benedict XVI declared that the remains were indeed those of the Apostle Paul. The sarcophagus area is now protected and a replica of the tombstone is in the Museum of the Ostian Way (Figure 144).

Lastly, one reason that Luke may not have finished Paul's story is that he may not have outlived the Apostle. In his second letter to Timothy, Paul states that most of his companions have deserted him and only Luke, "his beloved doctor" remains. Paul urges Timothy to come and be with him in Rome. Timothy did indeed come to be with Paul, as eventually did Epaphroditus from Philippi. While in Rome, Epaphroditus became seriously ill, but ultimately recovered. In writing to the Philippians, Paul related his joy over Epaphroditus' recovery as God spared him from experiencing "sorrow after sorrow". Clearly the first sorrow Paul mentioned would have been Epaphroditus' death. But the second sorrow seems to indicate that Paul had already experienced a deep sorrow and a second one heaped upon the first would have been more than he could have borne. Given Paul's commitment to die for Christ, I do not believe the other sorrow was a reference to his imprisonment in Rome or even the announcement of judgment against him. Instead, it could very well refer to the recent death of his beloved traveling companion, the faithful doctor, Luke.

Jesus began his ministry in Galilee, preaching the Good News of God's Kingdom by quoting the Prophet Isaiah. He then ended his ministry on the cross in Jerusalem. Thirty years later, Paul, Jesus' chosen apostle to the Gentiles, concluded his ministry in Rome preaching the Gospel by also quoting Isaiah. Paul's ministry started in Damascus and Jerusalem and then spread to "the ends of the earth" (Acts 1:8). Both Jesus and Paul set out on risky journeys; both proclaimed the Good News that God's salvation was for all mankind; both were empowered by the Holy Spirit; both met deadly opposition and went to their death's obedient to God's word. In Luke's Gospel, he relays one of Jesus' greatest parables, that of the prodigal son (Luke 15:11-32). Never in the history of Christianity was there more of a prodigal son than Saul of Tarsus, who became the light of Christian belief to millions of followers to this day.

"For I am already being poured out like a drink offering, and the time for my departure is near. I have fought the good fight, I have finished the race, I have kept the faith. Now there is in store for me the crown of righteousness, which the Lord, the righteous Judge, will award to me on that day – and not only to me, but also to all who have longed for his appearing." (II Timothy 4:6-8)

ACKNOWLEDGEMENTS

The impetus for writing this book came almost immediately after returning from an extended visit to Israel, the Palestinian State and Jordan in the spring of 2016. I was so inspired after walking many of the sites from Jesus' time and His ministry in Palestine that I wanted to visit the sites involved in the spread of Christianity across the Roman world during the first century A.D. This led to two additional expeditions that included all the early Christian sites in Greece (Neopolis, Philippi, Thessalonica, Berea, Athens, the Areopagus, Cenchreae, Isthmia and Corinth) plus Ephesus in western Turkey, the islands of Patmos, Rhodes (including the Lindos Acropolis and St. Paul's Bay), Crete and Malta; and Rome. The planning and execution of most of these trips was due to my dear friend, Ms. Nanette Dawson of Adonde Travel in Houston (www.adondetravel.com) who listened to me talk about the places I wanted to visit (Biblical and Classical) and somehow managed to get them all included on an agenda. If I haven't said it before, thank you, thank, thank you, Nanette. If you are looking to do a Biblical tour of either Israel or Ancient Greece, you should definitely give Adonde Travel in Houston a call. I would also like to thank all the individuals and organizations who gave me their permission to reproduce some of their photographs herein. One of the benefits of having been a Global Manager in the Exxon Mobil Corporation was all the fantastic contacts and friends I have made over the years around the world. In planning this book, I realized that there were a number of "holes": places I wanted to write about but had never visited, and as a consequence, had no photos of them. I put out a general call to my colleagues, especially in the offices in Turkey, Italy, Greece, and elsewhere in Europe and Central Asia, and received a number of excellent photos which are included in this volume. I would also like to thank "On Wings of Eagles Christian Tours" of Brighton, Colorado for their permission to use several of their photos. Additionally, I would like to thank Mr. Denis P. Wolf and Dr. Carl Rasmussen (www.HolyLandPhotos.org) for permission to use some of their photos. I especially wish to thank my Houston Archeological Society colleagues, Louis Aulbach and Linda Gorski, who have written a number of walking tour books on Ancient Rome. They gladly shared some of their extensive photo collection to help me in this project. Louis also serves as my "publisher", taking my rough drafts and magically turning them into the beautifully illustrated volume you now posses. He has done this for all three of my books to date and he is the best of the best at self-publishing and a dear friend and archeological colleague as well. I would also like to thank Mr. Lance K. Trask, who illustrated the excellent maps contained in this volume. Lastly, I would like to thank my wife, Ginny, for her steadfast love and support throughout my life and my journey as a teacher of the Bible. Ginny painstakingly read, re-read and edited various drafts of the book and greatly improved its content with her comments. She is also responsible for many of the superior photographs of the ancient sites included in the book.

APPENDIX I
Possible Timeline of Paul's Missionary Journeys

- **Birth of Paul**   ca. 5 A.D. (?)

- **Paul travels to Jerusalem to study under**   ca. 18 A.D. (?)
  Gamaliel (age 13)

- **Paul persecutes the church in Jerusalem**   ca. 31-32 A.D.
  (Acts 7:54-8:3)

- **Conversion on the road to Damascus**   ca. 31-32 A.D.
  (Acts 9:1-31)

- **Paul goes to Arabia to contemplate his new**   ca. 32-35 A.D.
  mission in life (Galatians 1:17)

- **Paul returns briefly to Jerusalem and the goes**   ca. 35-40 A.D.
  home to Tarsus (Acts 9:26-30)

- **Antioch-on-the-Orontes; Paul preaches and**   ca. 40-46 A.D.
  prepares himself for his new mission
  (Acts 11:19-12:25)

- **First Missionary Journey**   ca. 46-47 A.D.
  Antioch-Antioch Pisidia-Iconium-Lystra-Derbe
  (Acts 13-14)

- **Council of Jerusalem**   ca. 49-50 A.D.
  (Acts 15; Galatians 2)

- **Second Missionary Journey**   ca. 50-52 A.D.
  Galatia-Troas-Philippi-Thessalonica-Berea-
  Athens-Corinth-Ephesus
  (Acts 15:30-18:23)

- **Third Missionary Journey**   ca. 54-57 A.D.
  Galatia-Ephesus (2+ years)-Macedonia-
  Greece-Jerusalem
  (Acts 19-21:15)

- **Paul arrested in Jerusalem; transferred to Caesarea;** ca. 57-60 A.D.
  imprisoned for two years; travels to Rome via
  Crete-Malta
  (Acts 21:16-28:16)

- **Paul in Rome; either executed in 62 A.D. or freed,**   ca. 60-67 A.D.
  re-arrested and executed sometime between 64-67 A.D.
  (Acts 28:17-31)

APPENDIX II
Suggested Biblical Archeology Readings

The list below is by no means meant to be a complete listing of the thousands of books one can read on various aspects of Paul's travels and ministry and the history and archeology of the cities he visited. I have selected those books which I consider to be some of the best references on the various subjects covered in this book for those who may wish to delve deeper into a particular area. Most of the below listed references can still be found in book stores and/or on sites such as Amazon.com.

Abrahamsen, Valerie A.
2009   *Women and Worship at Philippi: Diana, Artemis and Other Cults*. Yankee Clipper Books, Windsor Locks, Connecticut.

Akurgal, E.
1978   *Ancient Civilizations and Ruins of Turkey*. Haset Kitabevi, Istanbul.

Antonakis, Helen L. (Translator)
2003   *St. Paul the Apostle and Philippi and St. Lydia's Baptisery*. Prokopios, Philippi, Neapolis and Thassos.

Boldrini, Fabio and Niccolo Orsi Battaglini
2000   *All of Ancient Rome – Then and Now*. Casa Editrice Bonechi. Florence.

Braaten, Carl E. and Robert W. Jenson
2004   *Mary, Mother of God*. William B. Eerdmans Publishing, Grand Rapids. Michigan.

Browning, Iain
1982   *Jerash and the Decapolis*. Jordan Distribution Agency Ltd., Amman, in association with Chatto & Windus. London.

Buckert, Walter
1985   *Greek Religion*. Harvard University Press, Boston, Massachusetts.

Camp, J. M.
2001   *The Archeology of Athens*. Yale University Press, New Haven and London.

2003   *The Athenian Agora, A Short Guide to the Excavations of the Athenian Agora*. The American School of Classical Studies, Book No. 16, Athens.

Campbell, Duncan B.
2009   *Roman Auxiliary Forts, 27 B.C. – 378 A.D.* Osprey Publishing, Oxford.

Charalambos, Bakirtzis and Helmet Koester
1989   *Philippi at the Time of Paul and After His Death.* Wipf and Stock Publishers, Eugene, Oregon.

Cimak, F.
2004   *Journeys of Paul: From Tarsus to "The Ends of the Earth".* A. Turizm Yayinlan, Istanbul.

Cornfield, Gaalyah and David Noel Freedman, Editors
1976   *Archeology and the Bible: Book by Book.* Harper & Row Publishers. San Francisco.

Crook, Wilson W., III
2017   *The Peoples of the Bible.* CreateSpace, a DBA of On-Demand Publishing, LLC (an Amazon Company). Charleston, South Carolina.

D'Este, Sorita
2005   *Artemis – Virgin Goddess of the Sun and Moon.* Avalonia, Glastonbury.

Evren, A., D. Tuzun, A. Zulkagiroglu, P. Buyukkolanci, M. Buyukkolanci, C. Icten, E. Uchaylar, O. Yugruk, and B. Tuluk
2015   *Ephesus.* Dilam Yayinlari Press, Izmir.

Fant, C. E. and M. G. Reddish
2003   *A Guide to Biblical Sites in Turkey.* Oxford Press, Oxford.

Gates, Charles
2011   *Ancient Cities: The Archeology of Urban Life in the Ancient Near East, Egypt, Greece and Rome.* Routledge, New York.

Harding, G. Lankester
1967   *The Antiquities of Jordan* (Revised Edition). Jordan Distribution Company by arrangement with Lutterworth Press. Cambridge.

Johnson, Anne
1983   *Roman Forts of the 1st and 2nd Centuries A.D. in Britain and the German Provinces.* Adam and Charles Black, London.

King, Philip J. and Lawrence E. Stager
2001   *Life in Biblical Israel.* Westminster John Knox Press. Louisville and London.

Klawans, Zander H.
2012   *Handbook of Ancient Greek and Roman Coins.* Whitman Publishing LLC. Atlanta.

Korb, Scott
2010   *Life in Year One: What the World Was Like in First Century Palestine.* Riverhead
       Books. New York.

Mazar, Eilat
2002   *The Complete Guide to the Temple Mount Excavations.* Shoham Academic
Research and Publication. Jerusalem.

McRay, John
2001   *Archeology & The New Testament,* Fourth Edition. Baker Books, Grand Rapids.

Meinardus, Otto F. A.
1972   *St. Paul in Greece.* Lycanettus Press, Athens.

Murphy-O'Connor, Jerome
1971   *St. Paul's Ephesus.* Liturgical Press, Collegeville, Minnesota.

Mousteraki, Reghina
2015   *Apostle Paul: In the Footsteps of Apostle Paul, His Travels in Greece-Cyprus-   Asia
Minor-Rome.* Imagico Press Ltd., Athens.

Nichols, Matthew (Editor)
2014   *30-Second Ancient Rome.* Metro Books, New York.

Papahatzis, Nicos
2000   *Ancient Corinth: The Museums of Corinth, Isthmia and Sicyon.* Ekdotike Athenon,
S.A., Athens.

Rogers, Guy Maclean
2012   *The Mysteries of Artemis of Ephesos.* Yale University Press, New Haven,
       Connecticut.

Rose, J. J.
1959   *A Handbook of Greek Mythology.* E. P. Dutton, Boston, Massachusetts.

Sacks, David and Murray Oswyn
2009   *Encyclopedia of the Ancient Greek World.* Infobase Publishing, New York.

Scarre, Chris
1995   *Chronicles of the Roman Emperors.* Thames and Hudson, Ltd. London.

Shanks, Hershel, Editor
2011   *Ancient Israel from Abraham to the Roman Destruction of the Temple,* Third
       Edition. Biblical Archeology Society. Washington, D.C.

Themelis, Petros G.
1984   *Ancient Corinth: The Site and the Museum*. Editions Hanibal, Athens.

Walker, Peter
2008   *In the Steps of Saint Paul*. Lion Hudson plc., Oxford.

Wilson, Ian
1999   *The Bible Is History*. Weidenfield & Nicholson. London.

Wright, G. Ernest
1962   *Biblical Archeology*, Second Edition. The Westminster Press, Philadelphia and Gerald Duckworth and Company, Ltd., London.

1974   *Great People of the Bible and How They Lived*. The Reade's Digest Association, Inc. Pleasantville, New York.

ABOUT THE AUTHOR

Wilson W. Crook, III

Wilson W. "Dub" Crook, III retired after a 35 year distinguished career as a Senior Executive with the Exxon Mobil Corporation. Dub has traveled extensively all over the world, starting his archeological adventures as a child accompanying his father, Wilson W. "Bill" Crook, Jr., who was past President and Fellow of the Texas Archeological Society. As a result of his father's lifelong interest in archeology and paleoanthropology, Dub grew up going to and working on archeological and early man sites all around the world. A native of the Dallas area, Dub attended Highland Park High School and Southern Methodist University (SMU) where he majored in Geology (Mineralogy). He is the author of over 180 professional papers in such varied fields as archeology, mineralogy, geology, natural science and Soviet manned space exploration. Dub is a Life Member of the Dallas Archeological Society, a Fellow of the Houston Archeological Society, a long-time member of the Texas Archeological Society, a member of the Center for the Study of First Americans, a Life Member of the Gault School of Archeological Research, a Research Fellow at the Texas Archeological Research Laboratory in Austin, and a Fellow of the Leakey Foundation. Recently he was named an Archeological Steward for the State of Texas. He is also a long-time member of First Presbyterian Church of Kingwood and has been teaching Adult Sunday School lessons combining archeology and history with the scriptures for 30 years.

85108222R00108

Made in the USA
Lexington, KY
29 March 2018